Copyright © 2017 by Shoreline Publishing Group LLC

All rights reserved. Published by Scholastic Inc., *Publishers since 1920.*
SCHOLASTIC and associated logos are trademarks and/or registered trademarks of Scholastic Inc.

ISBN 978-1-338-03277-2

10 9 8 7 6 5 4 3 2   17 18 19 20

Printed in the U.S.A.   40
First edition, December 2016

Produced by Shoreline Publishing Group LLC

Due to the publication date, records, results, and statistics are current as of August 2016.

Contents

Titanic Teams!

Teamwork. Is there any more important word in sports? Just about every single athlete in this book played for a team of one sort or another. In 2016, we watched the members of national Olympic teams as they chased gold at the Summer Olympics in Rio de Janeiro (page 20). As the samba music played in the first Olympics ever held in South America, even the swimmers who swam alone or the wrestlers who wrestled solo were part of their nation's teams in the Games.

You can see the theme of teamwork throughout this edition of *YEAR IN SPORTS*. We marveled as the Golden State Warriors set a record with 73 wins, only to gasp as another NBA team, the Cleveland Cavaliers, stormed to the title.

We watched as the Kansas City Royals finally made their dream come true, using every player on the roster to win the World Series for the first time.

A team that few thought would end up on top did just that at the men's NCAA basketball championship. Villanova won it all on a three-point basket, but it was the pass from a teammate that made the shot possible.

On the women's side, the University of Connecticut was once again the team to beat . . . but no one could! They went undefeated while winning their record 11th title . . . together.

The Super Bowl was billed as a contest between the great quarterbacks **Peyton Manning** of the Broncos and

Kevin Harvick drove alone, but won as a team!

The US women's basketball team celebrated after winning its sixth straight gold medal.

Cam Newton of the Panthers. While both did well, it was Denver's defense that ended up dominating and making the Broncos the champions.

In soccer, no team played better together than Leicester City of the Premier League. Its players believed in themselves when no one else did . . . and they won!

But not everything people play is a team sport, right? What about golf, you say? Just ask LPGA star and two-time major winner **Lydia Ko** if she could have won without her caddie or her coach. Tennis? Even the great **Serena Williams** credits her "team" of supporters, family, and friends with inspiring her to greatness. Check out her win at Wimbledon on page 170. Auto racing? Sure, drivers like 2015 NASCAR champ **Kevin Harvick** (page 130) are alone in their cars, but good luck to them if they had to change their tires, too!

It even took a team of people to put together this book. And, of course, it takes all of you on the team of awesome sports fans to read it!

See? It's all about teamwork!

TOP 10

MOMENTS IN SPORTS
SEPTEMBER 2015 ▶ AUGUST 2016

In sports this past year, rings were the thing. The five Olympic rings capped off 12 months of ring-producing championships. Many of the winners were big surprises, which, of course, is one of the great things about sports. A team might set an all-time record for wins during the season, but lose in the championship game. *(Yes, we're talking about you, Warriors!)* Or a team might come out of nowhere to win a title that no one thought was possible. *(Hello, Leicester City!)* Then again, another team might dominate just as expected to add to a long string of rings. *(Huskies rule!)*

Some of sports' most memorable moments don't come with championships, however, but with amazing farewells *(60 points for Kobe!)* and Cinderella stories *(Iceland did what?)*. Sometimes, no one can believe the ending. *(Could the final seconds of the NCAA men's basketball title game have been any more dramatic? Wow!)*

Of course, there were lots more than 10 memorable moments in this year in sports—we don't have room for everything—but we hope that these memories "ring" a bell.

10 KOBE'S BIG NIGHT *The NBA and Lakers fans everywhere said good-bye to superstar Kobe Bryant in 2016. The 18-time All-Star retired as the NBA's third-leading scorer and as the owner of five NBA championship rings. He gave his fans one final amazing memory, racking up 60 points in his final game, the highest single-game total for any NBA player in the 2015–16 season.*

9 **GRAND SERENA** In 2015, *Serena Williams* fell one tournament short of capturing her first single-year Grand Slam. Then she lost in upsets at the 2016 Australian and French Opens. Finally, at Wimbledon, she broke her mini-losing streak by winning her seventh Wimbledon championship. That also gave her 22 Grand Slam championships for her career, tying Germany's *Steffi Graf* for the second-most all-time.

8 ICELAND! *Iceland didn't win a championship, but it sure won a lot of hearts and fans. The ultra-underdog shocked the soccer world by advancing to the quarterfinals of the European Championships. First, the Icelanders surprised everyone by winning their group, helped by an "upset" tie against Portugal. Then, in the knockout rounds, they handed England a stunning 2–1 defeat! The Icelanders' "Viking Chant" rocked the house until they finally lost to host country France. Portugal won the tournament.*

7

FOUR-PEAT! *It's one thing to repeat as champions. It's quite another to do it four times in a row! The Connecticut Huskies became the first four-peat champs in women's college hoops history. For the third time, UConn's Breanna Stewart (with ball) was chosen as the national player of the year (and in April 2016 she was the obvious choice as the WNBA's No. 1 draft pick!). It was the 11th title overall for UConn coach Geno Auriemma, giving him more championships in the sport than any other men's or women's coach.*

6

BRONCOS . . . BUSTERS!
Superstar quarterback Peyton Manning went out a winner, as his Denver Broncos beat the Carolina Panthers 24–10 to win Super Bowl 50. The offensive power of Panthers quarterback Cam Newton was supposed to be the story, but Denver's defense shut him down. Manning, the NFL's all-time leader in many key passing statistics, announced his retirement in the spring.

5

BASEBALL ROYALTY *After coming oh-so-close in 2014 (the Royals left the game-tying run on third base in Game 7), Kansas City sealed the deal in 2015 against the New York Mets, winning the World Series in five games. The clincher came thanks to a game-tying, ninth-inning rally—first baseman Eric Hosmer (35) celebrated after scoring the tying run—and a stack of 5 runs in the 12th inning. It was the eighth time in 2015 that the Royals came from behind to win a postseason game.*

DAKTRONICS

00.0

4 AT THE BUZZER!

For only the second time ever, the NCAA men's basketball title was decided on a buzzer-beating basket. Villanova's Kris Jenkins launched a three-point shot as the clocked ticked to 0:00. The ball swished through the net, and the Wildcats surprised favored North Carolina with a 77–74 win. It was the school's second title; the first came way back in 1985.

NCAA FINAL FOUR
HOUSTON 2016

3

OUT OF NOWHERE *There are long shots . . . and then there are loooonnnng shots! When the 2015–16 English Premier League soccer season began, the odds were 5,000-to-1 that Leicester City would win the title. Well, the team shocked the world by doing just that. It was one of the most surprising results in soccer history. Jamie Vardy was a star for the Foxes, setting a league record by scoring in 11 consecutive games.*

2

KING JAMES! *With the hopes of more than 2 million folks in Cleveland on his shoulders, and facing the winningest team in NBA history, forward LeBron James came through. He led the Cavaliers to a shocking NBA championship. They became the first team to win the title after trailing three games to one in the NBA Finals. James and guard Kyrie Irving each scored 41 points in Game 6. Then James had a triple-double and this game-saving block in the final moments of Game 7. For the first time ever, Cavs = Champs!*

ALL-TIME BEST *In his fifth Olympics, Michael Phelps earned more medals than any other swimmer, with five golds and a silver. But winning the most medals is nothing new for him. He wrapped up the greatest Olympic career ever with 28 total medals, including 23 gold. Both totals are way more than any other Olympian!*

1 SIMONE SOARS! *The superstar of the Rio Olympic Games was American gymnast Simone Biles. Already the winner of three all-around world championships, she dominated her sport in Rio. Biles won the all-around gold medal by nearly two points in a sport in which one-tenth of a point can be the deciding margin. Biles helped the American women win the team gold medal, too. Then she earned additional golds in the floor exercises and the vault, plus a bronze on the balance beam.*

2016 SUMMER OLYMPICS

COLOR THE WORLD!

The Opening Ceremonies of the 2016 Summer Olympics in Rio de Janeiro featured a worldwide rainbow of colors. The teams of 207 countries (or groups, see page 23) paraded into the Maracanã Stadium wearing their national colors. The uniforms, flags, and entertaining dancers covered the arena floor on the day before the world's athletes covered Rio in sports!

Golden Samba in Rio

The Summer Olympic Games in Brazil were not perfect, but the Brazilians sure tried hard! After fears of the water in the bay being horrible, swimming and sailing events came off almost without a hitch. A wildfire near the mountain biking course was kept under control. And the green diving pool? That made for some funny pictures (page 31), but the problem was quickly fixed. All the hassles went away, though, when Brazil won the men's soccer gold medal. It was their first in the sport they love best, and made goal-scoring **Neymar Jr.** an even bigger hero than he already was!

For the American team, the biggest moment in the 2016 Olympics came in 1972. That's the year the US government passed a new law called Title IX. It said that schools needed to give men and women equal treatment in sports. Since then, women's sports in America have skyrocketed.

US women earned 61 medals in Rio, and the men 55 (see page 32 for the full medal report). If the US women were their own country, they would have finished third in the medal count! Their 27 golds would have tied for the most with Great Britain!

The women gymnasts were among the American team's biggest stars. Led by all-around champ **Simone Biles**, they won the team all-around medal. Then, the gymnasts

The US won gold in rowing's "eights," just one of many triumphs for American women.

Neymar Jr. scored the golden goal.

REFUGEE TEAM

It's been a hard few years for some athletes. Their home countries are in turmoil and they've had to flee for their lives. But they still had Olympic dreams. By creating the Refugee Team, the Olympic Committee gave them the chance. Ten athletes from countries such as Syria, South Sudan, and Congo did their best, even if they didn't have a home to return to.

added eight individual medals. It was the last Olympics for longtime US coach **Márta Károlyi**, and the last time that five women will represent a country in the Olympics. (It goes to four in 2020.) So the young champions became "The Final Five."

American swimmers also dominated. Together, they earned 33 medals, which was 23 more than Australia, the second-place finisher. American swimmers won half of the possible gold medals, led as usual by **Michael Phelps**. **Simone Manuel** became the first African American swimmer to capture an individual gold medal. Manuel got her second gold when the women's medley relay team won, earning the United States its 1,000th gold medal since the modern Olympics began in 1896!

On the track, the big name was **Usain Bolt**. The amazing Jamaican sprinter reached a total of nine career gold medals! With a gold in the 4x400 relay, American sprinter **Allyson Felix** earned her ninth career medal, too (though not all gold). That ties her for most ever on the track by a female athlete! **Ashton Eaton** of the US won his second straight decathlon gold. The "world's greatest athlete" has an athletic house. His wife, **Brianne Theisen-Eaton**, won bronze for Canada in the heptathlon!

Most athletes earned glory by winning in spectacular fashion. Some got headlines for being another kind of good. An example? In the women's 5,000-meter race, American **Abbey D'Agostino** and New Zealander **Nikki Hamblin** collided and fell to the track. Instead of being angry, they helped each other up. Both were injured, but encouraged each other to try to finish the race. They won an award for their sportsmanship.

The Olympics in Rio were packed with color, music, samba dancing, and stunning athletes. We can't tell all their stories, but we hope we've included your favorites!

61

Medals by US female Olympians, which was more than any other countries' total except for China (70) and Great Britain (67).

Memorable Moments

▲GREATEST OLYMPIAN EVER

Michael Phelps already had that title, and he added to it in Rio. Phelps dominated the swimming events again, leading all swimmers with five gold medals (plus a silver!). His six total medals were the most by any athlete in Rio, and gave him an astonishing career total of 28 medals overall, including 23 golds. Both are all-time records by a wide margin. By winning the 200m individual medley, he also became the first swimmer ever to win the same event four times.

SWIM STAR

Katie Ledecky was so far ahead at the end of the 800m freestyle race that she could have gotten out of the pool and dried off before the second-place finisher arrived. Being out front was a theme for the 19-year-old from Maryland.

TEAM TRIUMPHS

Women's basketball: US over Spain

This gold medal was not a surprise at all. The US women's hoops team won its sixth straight gold and 49th straight Olympic game. **Diana Taurasi** set an Olympic record for three-point baskets along the way.

Men's basketball: US over Serbia ▶▶▶

The US squad of NBA veterans led by **Kevin Durant** (right) had some surprisingly close games early in the tournament. In the final, however, the US swamped Serbia by 30 points. **Carmelo Anthony** became America's all-time leading scorer in Olympic play.

Women's water polo: US over Italy

What a win! The US women set records for most goals scored and became the first-ever back-to-back gold medal winners.

Aly, Madison, Laurie, Simone, and Gabby take a bite out of their all-around team gold medals!

FINAL FIVE!

Simone **BILES**	🥇🥇🥇🥇🥉
Aly **RAISMAN**	🥇🥇🥇
Laurie **HERNANDEZ**	🥇🥇
Madison **KOCIAN**	🥇🥇
Gabby **DOUGLAS**	🥇

She became the first woman since 1968 to win the 200, 400, and 800m freestyle races at the same Olympics. She also won gold in the 4x200m freestyle relay. Add in a silver in the 4x100m relay, and that's a pretty amazing week.

FASTEST MAN ALIVE!

It's one thing to brag that you're the greatest. It's another to keep backing it up over and over again. Before the Games, Jamaica's **Usain Bolt** said that he'd win again . . . and he did. He became the first person ever to win the 100-meter race three times. Then he topped that by winning his third consecutive Olympic 200-meter race and by helping Jamaica win the 4x100 relay. Bolt went home with an amazing nine career gold medals!

STUNNING SIMONE!

With three all-around world championships,

Simone Biles was already considered one of the greatest gymnasts. With her amazing four gold medals in Rio—the most ever at one Olympics by an American in her sport—she can put away the "one of." She's simply the best! She won the all-around by almost two points, which doesn't sound like much. But if you add up the winning margins of the past seven Olympics, they don't equal two points. She was part of the US gold-medal "Final Five" team champions, and earned America's first gold in the vault. Then she added gold in the floor exercises and bronze on the beam. Wow!

More American Stars

A win by Maroulis (in blue) was an American first.

to take part in the Games wearing a hijab. That is the scarf-like head covering worn by devout Muslim women. An expert in the sabre, she lost to a French fencer in an early round. In the team event, she helped the US women win a bronze medal!

Three for the Road:
Kristin Armstrong won her third consecutive gold medal in the cycling time trial event. She tied speed skater Bonnie Blair as the only American women to win three golds in the same event.

On Point: Daryl Homer won a
silver medal in the sabre fencing event. It was the first American medal in this sport in 32 years. In 1984, a bronze medal in sabre fencing was won by Peter Westbrook . . . who went on to found a fencing school in New York City . . . where Daryl learned to fence!

Good Start: The first medal awarded at
the Rio Games went to 19-year-old Ginny Thrasher. Though ranked 23rd in the world, she won the 10-meter air rifle event in a huge upset. She became the youngest person ever to win the Games' first medal.

Groundbreaker I: Or should that be
"Pool-Breaker"? Simone Manuel won the women's 100m freestyle and became the first African American woman to win an individual swimming event. "This medal's not just for me, but for a whole bunch of people who came before and have been an inspiration to me," she said afterward. Manuel added gold in the medley relay and a pair of silver medals.

Groundbreaker II: Fencer Ibtihaj
Muhammad became the first US athlete

Slam!: Kayla Harrison won her second
straight 78-kg judo gold medal, a first for an American "judoka." Some experts say to look for her in MMA fights in the future.

Mat Magic: Helen Louise Maroulis
became the first American woman to win a gold medal in wrestling. All she had to do was defeat three-time Olympic champ and 13-time world champ Saori Yoshida. The huge upset also earned Maroulis a $250,000 bonus from USA Wrestling.

Muhammad really made her point!

More from the Pool:

➔ **Ryan Murphy** became the fifth American swimmer to win both the 100m and 200m backstroke golds in the same Olympics.

➔ **Maya DiRado** upset triple gold medalist **Katinka Hosszú** in the 200m backstroke. DiRado wound up with four medals overall.

➔ At 35, **Anthony Ervin** was the oldest swimming gold medalist ever after winning the 50m freestyle.

Six Shooter: Kim Rhode won

her sixth consecutive Olympic medal in shooting. She won her first three in double trap, and her second three in skeet shooting. Three of those were gold. In Rio, she won a four-person shoot-off to capture a bronze medal in skeet shooting and become the first person to win an Olympic medal on five different continents! (She won every year from 1996 to 2016—check online to find the continents of those six Olympic Games.)

Role Model: **Michelle Carter** won the shot put competition. She hopes to use her new fame to encourage girls to love themselves and their bodies, no matter what shape they are!

Track Stars

Some US highlights from track-and-field:

➔ 100m hurdles: **Brianna Rollins**, **Nia Ali**, and **Kristi Castlin** became the first American women ever to sweep all the medals in a single event.

➔ Long jump: **Tianna Bartoletta** and **Brittney Reese** took the top spots.

➔ Men's 800: **Clayton Murphy** was a surprise bronze medalist in this difficult, two-lap race.

➔ Men's 1500: **Matt Centrowitz** shocked the experts by becoming the first American man since 1908 to win this famous race.

➔ Women's 1500: **Jennifer Simpson**'s bronze was the first medal ever in this event for an American woman.

Centrowitz broke a 108-year losing streak.

Stars of the World

Hungary for Gold: Swimmer **Katinka Hosszú** won three gold medals. She won gold in the 100m backstroke and helped her country win the 400m IM and 200m IM relays. Toss in a silver in the 200m back and she was the top woman swimmer in Rio not named Katie!

Hometown Heroes:

Brazilians came out in force to cheer for their local heroes.

➡ The biggest roar of the Olympics came when **Neymar Jr.** slammed home the penalty kick that earned Brazil's men's team the gold in soccer. The international superstar also scored on a free kick during the game against Germany, which went to a shootout after a 1–1 tie. Brazil had never won Olympic gold in soccer.

➡ **Rafaela Silva** captured the first gold for Brazil in Rio, winning the 57kg judo event.

➡ **Thiago Braz da Silva** ▶▶▶ won the country's first-ever gold in the pole vault. He set an Olympic record by soaring 19 feet, 9.25 inches!

➡ Two Brazilian men won gymnastics silver medals: **Diego Hypólito** in floor exercise and **Arthur Zanetti** on the rings.

➡ **Alison** and **Bruno** won the beach volleyball gold medal, thrilling the samba-dancing fans that packed the ocean-side court.

On Target: South Korea swept the team archery gold medals. The women won for the eighth straight time. The men defeated the US in the gold-medal match. In that final, the Koreans shot 18 arrows—15 of them were right in the 10-point bulls-eye!

GGOAT?: That stands for Greatest Gymnast of All Time. That's what experts call Japan's **Kohei Uchimara**. He won his second straight gold in the men's all-around, after leading Japan to the team title. He has also won

Fiji's rugby gold medal set off a national celebration.

six straight world championships. His latest gold came by .099 points over Ukraine's **Oleg Verniaiev**.

Four!: **Kaori Icho** of Japan became the first wrestler, man or woman, to win four gold medals in an event. She captured the 58kg gold with a scoring move in the last seconds of the final match.

Welcome Back!: For the first time since 1904, golf was an Olympic sport. Great Britain's **Justin Rose** won the gold medal in the men's event. The women's champion was **Inbee Park** of South Korea.

Game, Set, Match, Repeat: Great Britain's **Andy Murray** became the first tennis player to repeat as Olympic champion. He beat Argentina's **Juan Martín del Potro** to match his gold-medal performance from London in 2012.

Really Great Briton!: **Laura Trott** won another gold medal in cycling, becoming the first female athlete from that country with four career golds!

First Timers!:

➔ After taking part in the Olympics since 1956, Fiji finally won its first medal. As its fans chanted and danced in the stands, Fiji won the first rugby sevens event, crushing Great Britain 43–7 in the final.

➔ **Xuan Vinh Hoang** became an instant celebrity . . . in Vietnam! He won the 10m air pistol event and claimed his nation's first Olympic gold medal ever. He later added a silver in the 50m event.

➔ Swimmer **Joseph Schooling** won Singapore's first gold medal ever.

➔ In women's tennis, **Monica Puig** shocked world No. 2 **Angelique Kerber** to win gold for Puerto Rico!

➔ In women's 52kg judo, **Majlinda Kelmendi** won Kosovo's first gold.

A sequence of Uchimara on the high bar.

O Canada

Tough Women: Canada beat Great Britain 33–10 to win a bronze in the first-ever Olympic women's rugby event.

Maple Leaf Bounce: Rosie MacLennan won her second consecutive gold in trampoline gymnastics.

Pinned!: Erica Wiebe grappled her way to gold in the 75kg freestyle wrestling class.

▼Hi, Jumper!: Derek Drouin became the first Canadian since 1932 to win the high jump gold, soaring 7 feet, 9¾ inches.

▲Teen Star!: Penny Oleksiak was the swimming star for Canada. She won four medals: gold (tied) in the 100m freestyle, silver in the 100m butterfly, and bronze in the 4x100 and 4x200 freestyle relays! Here's the cool part: She's only 16 years old!

Third-Fastest Man on Earth: Andre De Grasse finished behind the great Usain Bolt and American Justin Gatlin to earn bronze in the 100-meter dash. He also won silver in the 200 meters and bronze in the 4x100 relay.

Row, Row, Row . . . to Silver!: Lindsay Jennerich and Patricia Obee finished just about one second behind a team from the Netherlands to earn silver medals in the lightweight double scull event. A late charge took them all the way from fifth to second!

Fun and (Olympic) Games

A look at some of the more unusual and interesting news from the 2016 Olympics.

◀◀◀ A Medal . . . and a Ring, Times 2:

After China's He Zi won the silver in the women's springboard diving event, she was surprised by her boyfriend. Qin Hai, who had won a bronze of his own in synchronized diving, dropped to a knee and proposed marriage right on the medal platform! As fans cheered, Zi said yes! American triple jumper Will Claye did the same for his girlfriend, hurdler Queen Harrison . . . another yes!

Can we get a ruling? ▶▶▶:

The brand-new Olympic golf course attracted thousands of fans and some of the world's best golfers. It was also popular with a local capybara, a large species of rodent.

Two-Sport Star:

Nate Ebner had to hurry home from Rio. He played for the US in the first-ever rugby sevens competition, but his real job awaited him. Ebner is a defensive back with the New England Patriots!

The Lucky Hair Tie:

American runner Emma Coburn needed a hair tie for her 3000m steeplechase run. Fellow US runner Evan Jager lent one to her, then Emma won a bronze medal. It was the first by an American woman ever. The next day, Evan wore the same hair tie as he burst to a silver medal, the best finish by an American man since 1952. Was it the hair tie?

◀◀◀ St. Patrick's Day?:

On August 9, shocked divers showed up to practice but found that the water in their pool had turned bright green. "Is it for St. Patrick's Day?" one diver joked. It turned out that the wrong cleaning chemicals had been used. The water was safe, but it was drained and replaced.

Olympic Lists

2016 MEDAL STANDINGS

Here are the top countries in the 2016 total medal standings. The US total of 121 was the most in its history.

COUNTRY	GOLD	SILVER	BRONZE	TOTAL
UNITED STATES	46	37	38	121
CHINA	26	18	26	70
GREAT BRITAIN	27	23	17	67
RUSSIA	19	18	19	56
GERMANY	17	10	15	42
FRANCE	10	18	14	42
JAPAN	12	8	21	41
AUSTRALIA	8	11	10	29
ITALY	8	12	8	28
CANADA	4	3	15	22
SOUTH KOREA	9	3	9	21
NETHERLANDS	8	7	4	19
BRAZIL	7	6	6	19
NEW ZEALAND	4	9	5	18
AZERBAIJAN	1	7	10	18
SPAIN	7	4	6	17
KAZAKHSTAN	3	5	9	17

WORLD RECORDS!

Here are some of the new world records set at the 2016 Summer Games.

ATHLETE, COUNTRY	EVENT	RECORD
Almaz AYANA, Ethiopia	**10,000 Meters**	29:17.45
Katinka HOSSZÚ, Hungary	**400M Individual Medley**	4:26.36
Katie LEDECKY, United States	**800M Freestyle**	8:04.79
Katie LEDECKY, United States	**400M Freestyle**	3:56.46
Wayde VAN NIEKERK, South Africa	**400 Meters**	43.03 SECS
Adam PEATY, Great Britain	**100M Breaststroke**	57.13 SECS
Sarah SJÖSTRÖM, Sweden	**100M Butterfly**	55.48 SECS
Anita WLODARCZYK, Poland	**Hammer Throw**	269.9 FT
Deng WEI, China	**Weightlifting (63kg, Total)**	577.6 LBS
Kim WOO-JIN, South Korea	**Archery (Indiv.)**	700 PTS
AUSTRALIA (Women)	**4x100M Freestyle**	3:30.65
GREAT BRITAIN (Women)	**Cycling Team Pursuit**	4:10.236

UP NEXT! Tune in for these scheduled upcoming Olympic Games!

2018	Winter Olympics	PYEONGCHANG, SOUTH KOREA
2020	Summer Olympics	TOKYO, JAPAN
2022	Winter Olympics	BEIJING, CHINA

Note: In 2020, some great new sports, including surfing and skateboarding, will be added to the Olympics, while baseball and softball will return!

GOING OUT A WINNER
Denver quarterback Peyton Manning enjoys his final shining moment in the NFL sun. The future Hall of Famer led the Broncos to a 24–10 win over the Carolina Panthers in Super Bowl 50. A month later, Manning announced that he was retiring after a remarkable 18-year career.

NFL

Another Super Season!

Every NFL season is a mix of a little bit old, a little bit new. In 2015, fans enjoyed more of that same formula. Two of the "final four" teams had played in and won multiple Super Bowls. The other two were looking for their first taste of a Super Bowl victory. The veteran teams were led by superstar quarterbacks: New England's **Tom Brady** and Denver's **Peyton Manning**. The newbies boasted the NFL's hottest young signal caller, **Cam Newton** of Carolina, along with a player reaching long-sought potential, Arizona's **Carson Palmer**.

The road to reaching that final four, and eventually Super Bowl 50, was filled with the usual ups and downs. The NFC's Panthers made the biggest splash, losing only one game in the regular season. Also in the NFC, Minnesota surprised many experts by winning the North. The return of rampaging running back **Adrian Peterson** was a key to the Vikings' success. Washington squeaked into the NFC East title as the Giants and Eagles faltered. When the Cardinals won the NFC West, the Seattle Seahawks settled for a wild-card playoff berth, along with the Green Bay Packers.

In the AFC, Cincinnati looked like the team to beat for a while. The Bengals won the North, but an injury to QB **Andy Dalton** probably doomed their Super Bowl hopes. Defensive player of the year **J. J. Watt** led the Houston Texans back to the playoffs as the South champs. The AFC East-champion Patriots equaled an NFL record when they won a division title for the seventh consecutive season. In the West, Denver won the division, but Kansas City put on the biggest show. The Chiefs were just 1–5 after six games, then reeled off a 10-game winning streak to earn a wild-card spot along with Pittsburgh.

One thing NFL fans always watch for is rising stars. A pair of young running backs made big marks on the league in 2015. Rams rookie **Todd Gurley** rushed for 125 or more yards in four of his first five games, an NFL first. The Falcons' **Devonta Freeman**, a second-year player, jumped into the starting lineup and

J. J. Watt was the NFL's top defender once again.

became one of the top fantasy players of the season. Quarterback **Jameis Winston**, the No. 1 draft pick in 2015, performed pretty well for Tampa Bay and showed the potential to be even better with experience.

Veteran stars still got headlines, too. Brady led the NFL in passing TDs. **Drew Brees** of New Orleans won his sixth passing yardage title. New England kicker **Stephen Gostkowski** led the league in scoring for a record-tying fifth season.

At the end of the season, it was "old" versus "new" in the Super Bowl, which celebrated its golden anniversary. Keep reading to relive the whole season and its memorable finish!

Rams Stampede LA!

In January 2016, the NFL announced that the St. Louis Rams were heading west. After 21 seasons without an NFL team, Los Angeles welcomed the return of a club that had left for nearby Anaheim in 1980, then moved to St. Louis in 1995. The "new" Los Angeles Rams were to play their 2016 games at the Los Angeles Memorial Coliseum. They are scheduled to move into a new, high-tech, ultra-cool stadium for the 2019 season.

2015 Final Regular-Season Standings

AFC EAST		NFC EAST	
New England Patriots	12–4	Washington Redskins	9–7
New York Jets	10–6	Philadelphia Eagles	7–9
Buffalo Bills	8–8	New York Giants	6–10
Miami Dolphins	6–10	Dallas Cowboys	4–12
AFC NORTH		**NFC NORTH**	
Cincinnati Bengals	12–4	Minnesota Vikings	11–5
Pittsburgh Steelers	10–6	Green Bay Packers	10–6
Baltimore Ravens	5–11	Detroit Lions	7–9
Cleveland Browns	3–13	Chicago Bears	6–10
AFC SOUTH		**NFC SOUTH**	
Houston Texans	9–7	Carolina Panthers	15–1
Indianapolis Colts	8–8	Atlanta Falcons	8–8
Jacksonville Jaguars	5–11	New Orleans Saints	7–9
Tennessee Titans	3–13	Tampa Bay Buccaneers	6–10
AFC WEST		**NFC WEST**	
Denver Broncos	12–4	Arizona Cardinals	13–3
Kansas City Chiefs	11–5	Seattle Seahawks	10–6
Oakland Raiders	7–9	St. Louis Rams	7–9
San Diego Chargers	4–12	San Francisco 49ers	5–11

2015 Playoffs

Wild-Card Playoffs

Chiefs 30, Texans 0

Knile Davis returned the opening kickoff for a touchdown, and it just kept getting better from there for the Chiefs. They won their first playoff game since 1994. Kansas City picked off 4 passes and recovered a fumble while winning its 11th consecutive game.

Steelers 18, Bengals 16

With the lead and the ball and only a little more than 90 seconds left, Cincinnati looked like it would finally break its playoff jinx. It didn't. **Jeremy Hill** fumbled, and Pittsburgh recovered. The Bengals still had a shot to hold onto the lead, but they collapsed. They committed two dumb penalties—a blow to the head and an unsportsmanlike conduct—leaving Pittsburgh's **Chris Boswell** with an easy, 35-yard field goal that gave the Steelers an unlikely win.

Seahawks 10, Vikings 9

With less than a minute left, Minnesota kicker **Blair Walsh** missed a 27-yard field goal that would have won the game. The shocking ending came in a game played in subzero weather. Both teams struggled to move the ball in the freezing conditions. It was the fewest points scored by a playoff winner since 1997.

The Seahawks overcame the Vikings—and the cold.

Packers 35, Redskins 18

After a slow start, the Packers rallied and won easily. **Aaron Rodgers** passed for 2 touchdowns, and **Eddie Lacy** and **James Starks** each ran for a touchdown. Green Bay's victory in Washington meant that—for the first time—all four road wild-card teams won their games.

Divisional Playoffs

Patriots 27, Chiefs 20

Rob Gronkowski caught 2 touchdown passes as New England earned its fifth straight trip to the AFC Championship Game. The catches gave Gronk 8 career postseason scores, an NFL record for a tight end. Kansas City's **Alex Smith** threw 50 passes, but it was not enough. The Chiefs' winning streak ended at 11 games.

Cardinals 26, Packers 20 (OT)

An instant classic! In a wild, back-and-forth game, Arizona took the lead late in the fourth quarter on a ball that was tipped by Green Bay to the Cardinals' **Michael Floyd**. But in the final seconds of the period, Packers quarterback **Aaron Rodgers** hit **Jeff Janis** with a 60-yard pass, then a 41-yard Hail Mary for a touchdown. Janis caught the ball as time ran out to tie the game. It was the first time an NFL postseason game was tied on the final play. On the first play of overtime, Arizona's **Larry Fitzgerald** caught a short pass and raced 75 yards to Green Bay's 5-yard line. He then took a shovel pass from **Carson Palmer** to score the game-winning TD. Wow!

Panthers 31, Seahawks 24

After about four minutes, the Panthers led 14–0. A few minutes later, the score was 24–0. By halftime, it was Panthers 31, Seahawks 0. Carolina's defense bothered Seattle QB **Russell Wilson** and picked off 2 passes, returning 1 for a score. The second half was another story. The Seahawks dominated, scoring 24 unanswered points. Their comeback fell

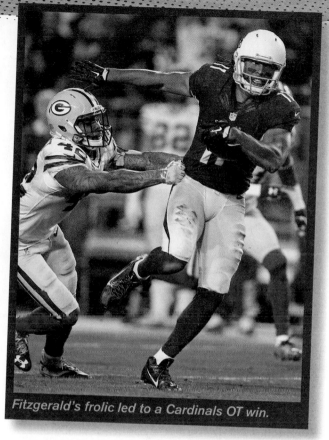
Fitzgerald's frolic led to a Cardinals OT win.

short, however. As their coach **Pete Carroll** said, "We ran out of time."

Broncos 23, Steelers 16

A late Pittsburgh fumble set up a touchdown drive that gave the Broncos the go-ahead score. It was the 55th time legendary Denver quarterback **Peyton Manning** led a late-game drive to victory. Broncos kicker **Brandon McManus** tied a playoff record with 5 field goals, which was even more impressive in Denver's swirling winds. The Broncos' victory put them in the AFC title game against New England—the 17th all-time meeting between Manning and Patriots QB **Tom Brady**.

Championship Games

Luke Kuechly's interception return for a touchdown capped the Panthers' win.

AFC

Broncos 20, Patriots 18

Denver's defense bottled up the powerful Patriots all afternoon, picking off **Tom Brady** twice and knocking him down a season-high 23 times! But Tom Terrific nearly pulled off a miracle. Only Denver's stop of a last-minute, 2-point try prevented New England from forcing overtime. The Broncos earned their record-tying eighth trip to the Super Bowl. **Peyton Manning** passed for 2 TDs in the game. At 39, he became the oldest starting quarterback to make it to the Super Bowl.

NFC

Panthers 49, Cardinals 15

Arizona entered the game leading the NFL in total yards. Carolina did not care at all, throttling the high-powered Cardinals in a record-setting performance. The Panthers forced QB **Carson Palmer** into 6 of Arizona's 7 turnovers, including a pick-six by linebacker **Luke Kuechly**. On offense, the Panthers' **Cam Newton** was a touchdown machine. He ran for 2 scores and passed for 2 more. Carolina's 49 points set an NFC Championship Game record.

Super Bowl 50

The Broncos entered Super Bowl 50 with the top-ranked defense in the NFL. The Panthers countered with the highest-scoring offense. Add in the celebration of the Super Bowl's 50th game and the possibility that it would be the last for NFL legend **Peyton Manning**, and you have the recipe for a memorable battle.

But from almost the first series, the script for the game was set and didn't change much. Manning helped put the Broncos ahead for good by marching his team to a field goal on the opening drive. A few moments later, Denver's defense did its job. Linebacker **Von Miller** sacked Carolina quarterback **Cam Newton** and stripped the ball. Defensive end **Malik Jackson** recovered the fumble in the end zone, and

Miller had Newton's number.

SUPER BOWL 50					
TEAM	1Q	2Q	3Q	4Q	FINAL
CAROLINA	0	7	0	3	10
DENVER	10	3	3	8	24

SCORING

1Q: Den FG McManus 34

1Q: Den Jackson fumble recovery in end zone (McManus kick)

2Q: Car Stewart 1 run (Gano kick)

2Q: Den FG McManus 33

3Q: Den FG McManus 30

4Q: Car FG Gano 39

4Q: Den Anderson 2 run (Fowler pass from Manning)

Denver was up 10–0. Carolina managed a touchdown but was never really in the game. Miller and his mates were all over Newton, generating 7 sacks and applying constant pressure. Miller, the game's MVP, stripped Newton again late in the game to set up the final touchdown. Meanwhile, Manning did just enough to keep Denver's offense in the game, setting up **Brandon McManus** for 3 field goals. One of those came after **Jordan Norwood** set a Super Bowl record with a 61-yard punt return. (McManus set an NFL record for field goals without a miss in the postseason when he was 10 for 10.)

Newton had been named the NFL's regular-season MVP the night before, but on Super Bowl Sunday, he never seemed to get comfortable. His teammates didn't help, with several dropped passes and a fumble. Denver once again proved the old saying that "defense wins championships."

Stats Leaders

1,485 RUSHING YARDS
Adrian Peterson, Vikings

11 RUSHING TDs
Devonta Freeman, Falcons
Jeremy Hill, Bengals
Adrian Peterson, Vikings
DeAngelo Williams, Steelers

36 PASSING TDs
Tom Brady, Patriots ▼▼▼

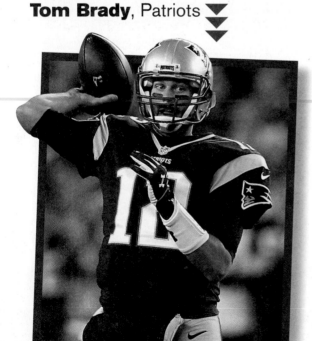

4,870 PASSING YARDS
Drew Brees, Saints

1,871 RECEIVING YARDS
Julio Jones, Falcons

136 RECEPTIONS
Julio Jones, Falcons
Antonio Brown, Steelers

14 RECEIVING TDs
Doug Baldwin, Seahawks
Brandon Marshall, Jets
Allen Robinson, Jaguars

34 FIELD GOALS
Blair Walsh, Vikings

151 POINTS
Stephen Gostkowski, Patriots

17.5 SACKS
J. J. Watt, Texans

8 INTERCEPTIONS
Reggie Nelson, Bengals
Marcus Peters, Chiefs

Award Winners

NFL MVP
OFFENSIVE PLAYER OF THE YEAR
CAM NEWTON QB ▶▶▶
PANTHERS

DEFENSIVE PLAYER OF THE YEAR
J. J. WATT DE
TEXANS

OFFENSIVE ROOKIE OF THE YEAR
TODD GURLEY RB
RAMS

DEFENSIVE ROOKIE OF THE YEAR
MARCUS PETERS CB
CHIEFS

COMEBACK PLAYER OF THE YEAR
ERIC BERRY S
CHIEFS

COACH OF THE YEAR
RON RIVERA
PANTHERS

WALTER PAYTON
NFL MAN OF THE YEAR AWARD
(FOR COMMUNITY SERVICE)
ANQUAN BOLDIN WR
49ERS

43

Okay, that's not a really "big" number. But consider this: That's the NFL record-tying number of rushing touchdowns by **Cam Newton**. It took **Steve Young** 15 years to reach that total. Cam reached it in five!

1st Quarter
WEEKS 1-4

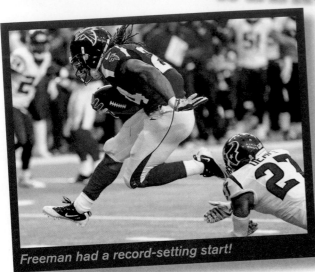

Freeman had a record-setting start!

✱ Deflate This: Tom Brady started for the Patriots after a judge lifted his four-game suspension. The NFL had said that Brady helped use illegal balls in the 2014 AFC Championship Game. The judge said the NFL's punishment was too much. Tight end **Rob Gronkowski** caught 3 of Brady's 4 touchdown passes. New England beat Pittsburgh 28–21.

✱ Not So Easy: Starting in 2015, the extra-point kick became a 33-yard try. Houston's **Randy Bullock** was the first kicker to miss the longer PAT.

✱ Oops, They Did It Again: The Seahawks ended the 2014 season with a mistake at the goal line that cost them the Super Bowl. They started the 2015 season with a mistake in overtime—a poorly executed onside kick—that also cost them a win. After scoring late in the fourth quarter to tie the game, the Rams won 34–31.

✱ Great Start!: Quarterback **Marcus Mariota**, the No. 2 overall pick in the draft, started his NFL career with a splash, throwing 4 touchdown passes in Tennessee's 42–14 win over Tampa Bay.

✱ Heisman Versus Heisman: Cleveland's **Johnny Manziel** and Tampa Bay's **Jameis Winston** led their teams to victory in Week 2. That marked the first time a pair of Heisman Trophy-winning quarterbacks won their first NFL games in the same weekend.

✱ Fireworks Timeout: The Steelers-Rams game in St. Louis in Week 3 started 30 minutes late after a pregame fireworks display lit part of the field on fire!

✱ OT Excitement: Three games needed extra time to find a winner in Week 4. The Ravens beat the Steelers 23–20 on **Justin Tucker's** 52-yard field goal….With fourth-year starting QB **Andrew Luck** missing a game for the first time in his NFL career, backup **Matt Hasselbeck** led the Colts to a 16–13 win over the Jaguars. . . . On Sunday night, New Orleans running back **C. J. Spiller** turned a pass from **Drew Brees** into an 80-yard TD romp on the second play of the extra period. The Saints won 26–20.

✱ Two for Three: Atlanta running back **Devonta Freeman** scored 3 touchdowns in the Falcons' 48–21 win over Houston. That followed 3 rushing TDs a week earlier. He was the first NFL player to score a trio of TDs in each of his first two career starts.

2nd Quarter
WEEKS 5-8

★ Hot Starts: Through the first five weeks of the season, six teams were undefeated: the Packers, Patriots, Panthers, Falcons, Broncos, and Bengals. It was the most no-loss teams ever at that point.

★ Falcons Fly!: Atlanta remained perfect in the season after a furious comeback tied its game against the Redskins on a 52-yard field goal. In overtime, **Robert Alford** scored on a 59-yard interception return to beat Washington 25–19.

★ Ring the Bell: On the final play of a game on Monday night against San Diego, Pittsburgh running back **Le'Veon Bell** took a snap from the 1-yard line in the "Wildcat" formation. He stuck the ball across the line as the clock read 0:00 to give the Steelers a 24–20 win.

Tannehill hit a record streak for Miami.

★ Third String a Charm: Pittsburgh was without starting quarterback **Ben Roethlisberger** in Week 6. Then backup **Michael Vick** pulled a muscle. In came third-stringer **Landry Jones**. He played like a starter, though, throwing a pair of TDs to **Martavis Bryant** and leading the Steelers to a 25–13 win over the Cardinals.

★ On Target: Miami QB **Ryan Tannehill** set an NFL record in the Dolphins' 44–26 win over Houston. He had completed his final 7 passes of Week 6, then hit 18 in a row to start Week 7. That made 25 consecutive completions, a new all-time best! Against the Texans, he had 4 TD passes. Miami led 41–0 before Houston staged a mini-comeback.

★ English Excitement: The Jaguars and Bills flew "across the pond" to play in London, and they gave English fans a jolly good show! Buffalo scored 18 points in the fourth quarter to take a late lead, but Jacksonville's **Blake Bortles** hit **Allen Hurns** for the go-ahead TD pass with just over two minutes left for a 34–31 win.

★ Lucky 13!: **Drew Brees** of the Saints became the eighth QB ever with 7 TD passes in one game. Playing against him, **Eli Manning** of the Giants had 6 scoring strikes. Their total of 13 was the most ever in an NFL game! New Orleans won 52–49 when **Kai Forbath** kicked a 50-yard field goal as time expired. The teams' combined total of 101 points equaled the third-most ever in an NFL game.

3rd Quarter
WEEKS 9-12

✱ Panther Power!: The surprising Carolina Panthers remained undefeated with a big victory over the Packers, 37–29.

✱ Lions Roar!: Detroit had not beaten the Packers in Green Bay since 1991. That streak ended thanks to a solid defensive effort that kept the Packers from scoring a game-tying 2-point conversion late. The Lions won 18–16.

✱ Bonus Play: Baltimore nearly had a win over Jacksonville on a sack of **Blake Bortles**. But a facemask penalty gave the Jaguars one more play, and they made it count. **Jason Myers** made a 53-yard field goal with no time on the clock for a surprise 22–20 victory.

✱ Home Wreckers: The Eagles won't want the Buccaneers to visit again. Tampa Bay crushed Philadelphia 45–17. **Jameis Winston** threw 5 TD passes, while **Doug Martin** ran for 235 yards. It was the first time an NFL road team had that many TD passes and a 200-yard runner in the same game!

✱ Unstoppable!: At 346 pounds, Kansas City defensive tackle

Dontari Poe became the heaviest player ever to score a rushing touchdown. He barreled over from the 1-yard line to open the scoring in the Chiefs' 33–3 win over San Diego.

✱ Surprise Star: **Marshawn Lynch** usually makes the news among Seattle running backs. But he was out with an injury, so backup **Thomas Rawls** stepped in—and took off! The free-agent rookie ran for 209 yards and scored 2 touchdowns as the 'Hawks beat the division-rival 49ers 29–13.

Winston leaped for joy!

✱ Illegal Shouting?: The Bengals were called for an odd unsportsmanlike-conduct penalty for shouting out fake signals near the end of their big game against the Cardinals. The 15-yard penalty gave Arizona kicker **Chandler Catanzaro** a much closer, 32-yard field-goal attempt. He made the kick to give his team a key 34–31 win.

✱ Kick Six?: Baltimore capped off a wild Monday-night game by scoring on a blocked field goal on the final play to beat Cleveland. Playing in his first NFL game, **Brent Urban** blocked the kick. Teammate **Will Hill** picked up the loose ball and raced 64 yards to give the Ravens a 33–27 win.

4th Quarter
WEEKS 13-17

★ Miracle in Motown: The Lions looked like they had the Packers beat. As the clock ran down to 0:00, though, a defensive penalty gave **Aaron Rodgers** one more shot. The Green Bay QB heaved a 61-yard rainbow toward the end zone. From a crowd of players, **Richard Rodgers** (no relation!) rose up to make the miraculous catch! Packers 27, Lions 23.

★ A Special Win: In the Eagles' 35–28 win over the mighty Patriots, Philadelphia returned a blocked punt for a touchdown, then the Eagles' **Malcolm Jenkins** returned an interception 99 yards for another. Add in **Darren Sproles**' 83-yard punt return for a TD, and it was enough for the upset win.

★ Tough Break: Cincinnati was hit by a key injury when QB **Andy Dalton** broke his right thumb while making a tackle on an interception return. With Dalton out, the Bengals fell 33–20 to Pittsburgh.

★ Cam Can!: The Panthers became the fourth NFL team ever to start 14–0. They needed late-game magic from **Cam Newton** to beat the Giants 38–35. Newton became the first NFL QB with 300 yards passing, 100 yards rushing, and 5 TD passes in one game!

★ Undefeated No More: The Panthers finally lost a game in Week 16. The Falcons, who had lost to Carolina 38–0 only a few weeks earlier, kept up the pressure on

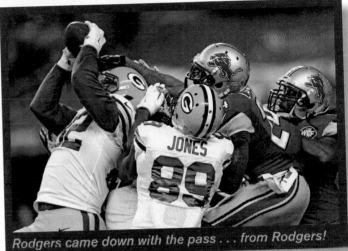

Rodgers came down with the pass . . . from Rodgers!

quarterback **Cam Newton** all game long. A 70-yard touchdown catch by **Julio Jones** in the third quarter gave the Falcons a lead they never gave up. Atlanta won 20–13.

★ OT Surprise: When a team wins the coin flip for overtime, it nearly always chooses to get the ball. After all, if it scores a touchdown, the game is over. When the Jets and Patriots tied 20–20, New England won the toss and captain **Matthew Slater** said, "Kick off." Even the ref sounded shocked, but Patriots coach **Bill Belichick** later said it was his decision. Oops. The Jets drove 80 yards and scored for the 26–20 upset.

★ KC Joy: The Chiefs became the first NFL team ever to lose five consecutive games and win nine consecutive games in one season. Their Week 16 win over Cleveland also vaulted them into the playoffs!

Milestones

★ **Julio Jones** of the Falcons became only the second player ever with 125 catches and 1,700 yards receiving in a season. Then **Antonio Brown** of the Steelers became the third! They were the first pair to top 135 receptions and 1,800 yards in the same season.

★ **Brandon Marshall** of the Jets became the first player with six seasons of 100 or more catches.

★ Carolina quarterback **Cam Newton** became the first player with 30 passing TDs and 8 rushing TDs in the same season.

★ Seattle QB **Russell Wilson** had a record-setting season as the first to top 4,000 passing yards, 30 passing TDs, and 500 rushing yards in one season. Wilson also had an NFL-record five consecutive games with 3 passing TDs and no interceptions.

★ Green Bay became the second NFL team with 750 all-time wins (including postseason games). The Packers joined the Chicago Bears in that small club.

★ The 194 receptions by Miami's **Jarvis Landry** in 2014 (84 catches) and 2015 (110 catches) were the most ever by a player in his first two seasons.

Gronk was a fantasy star.

FANTASY STARS

Here are the top-scoring players in season-long fantasy football, according to NFL.com:

POS.	PLAYER, TEAM	POINTS
QB	**Cam Newton**, Panthers	389.08
WR	**Antonio Brown**, Steelers	246.20
RB	**Devonta Freeman**, Falcons	243.40
TE	**Rob Gronkowski**, Patriots	183.60
K	**Stephen Gostkowski**, Patriots	159.00
DEF	**Denver Broncos**	175.00

2016 Hall of Fame

A large class of greats joined the Pro Football Hall of Fame in 2016.

Brett Favre QB ▶▶▶

(1991–2010) ◆ Won three NFL MVP awards and Super Bowl XXXI ◆ Retired as the NFL leader in passing yards, TDs, attempts, and completions ◆ Played 16 seasons with Green Bay before finishing his career with the Vikings and Jets

Marvin Harrison WR

(1996–2008) ◆ Third all-time with 1,102 career receptions ◆ Eight-time Pro Bowl selection

Kevin Greene DE/LB

(1985–1999) ◆ Third all-time with 160 career sacks ◆ Fast and furious pass rusher for four teams

Tony Dungy

(1996–2008) ◆ First African American to coach team to a Super Bowl title (Colts, XLI) ◆ Had only one losing season in 13 years leading the Colts and the Buccaneers

Ken Stabler QB

(1970–1984) ◆ Lefty passer guided the Raiders to Super Bowl XI win ◆ Career .661 winning percentage in regular-season games ◆ 1974 NFL MVP

Dick Stanfel OL

(1952–1958) ◆ Five-time Pro Bowl player ◆ Named to the NFL's official All-Decade Team of the 1950s

Orlando Pace OL

(1997–2009) ◆ Powerful run blocker for the Rams ◆ Named to seven Pro Bowls

Eddie DeBartolo

(1977–2000) ◆ Owner of 49ers teams that won five Super Bowls and played in 10 NFC Championship Games

For the Record

Super Bowl Winners

GAME	SEASON	WINNING TEAM	LOSING TEAM	SCORE	SITE
50	2015	**Denver**	Carolina	**24–10**	Santa Clara
XLIX	2014	**New England**	Seattle	**28–24**	Arizona
XLVIII	2013	**Seattle**	Denver	**43–8**	New Jersey
XLVII	2012	**Baltimore**	San Francisco	**34–31**	New Orleans
XLVI	2011	**NY Giants**	New England	**21–17**	Indianapolis
XLV	2010	**Green Bay**	Pittsburgh	**31–25**	North Texas
XLIV	2009	**New Orleans**	Indianapolis	**31–17**	South Florida
XLIII	2008	**Pittsburgh**	Arizona	**27–23**	Tampa
XLII	2007	**NY Giants**	New England	**17–14**	Arizona
XLI	2006	**Indianapolis**	Chicago	**29–17**	South Florida
XL	2005	**Pittsburgh**	Seattle	**21–10**	Detroit
XXXIX	2004	**New England**	Philadelphia	**24–21**	Jacksonville
XXXVIII	2003	**New England**	Carolina	**32–29**	Houston
XXXVII	2002	**Tampa Bay**	Oakland	**48–21**	San Diego
XXXVI	2001	**New England**	St. Louis	**20–17**	New Orleans
XXXV	2000	**Baltimore**	NY Giants	**34–7**	Tampa
XXXIV	1999	**St. Louis**	Tennessee	**23–16**	Atlanta
XXXIII	1998	**Denver**	Atlanta	**34–19**	South Florida
XXXII	1997	**Denver**	Green Bay	**31–24**	San Diego
XXXI	1996	**Green Bay**	New England	**35–21**	New Orleans
XXX	1995	**Dallas**	Pittsburgh	**27–17**	Tempe
XXIX	1994	**San Francisco**	San Diego	**49–26**	South Florida
XXVIII	1993	**Dallas**	Buffalo	**30–13**	Atlanta

GAME	SEASON	WINNING TEAM	LOSING TEAM	SCORE	SITE
XXVII	1992	**Dallas**	Buffalo	**52–17**	Pasadena
XXVI	1991	**Washington**	Buffalo	**37–24**	Minneapolis
XXV	1990	**NY Giants**	Buffalo	**20–19**	Tampa
XXIV	1989	**San Francisco**	Denver	**55–10**	New Orleans
XXIII	1988	**San Francisco**	Cincinnati	**20–16**	South Florida
XXII	1987	**Washington**	Denver	**42–10**	San Diego
XXI	1986	**NY Giants**	Denver	**39–20**	Pasadena
XX	1985	**Chicago**	New England	**46–10**	New Orleans
XIX	1984	**San Francisco**	Miami	**38–16**	Stanford
XVIII	1983	**LA Raiders**	Washington	**38–9**	Tampa
XVII	1982	**Washington**	Miami	**27–17**	Pasadena
XVI	1981	**San Francisco**	Cincinnati	**26–21**	Pontiac
XV	1980	**Oakland**	Philadelphia	**27–10**	New Orleans
XIV	1979	**Pittsburgh**	Los Angeles	**31–19**	Pasadena
XIII	1978	**Pittsburgh**	Dallas	**35–31**	Miami
XII	1977	**Dallas**	Denver	**27–10**	New Orleans
XI	1976	**Oakland**	Minnesota	**32–14**	Pasadena
X	1975	**Pittsburgh**	Dallas	**21–17**	Miami
IX	1974	**Pittsburgh**	Minnesota	**16–6**	New Orleans
VIII	1973	**Miami**	Minnesota	**24–7**	Houston
VII	1972	**Miami**	Washington	**14–7**	Los Angeles
VI	1971	**Dallas**	Miami	**24–3**	New Orleans
V	1970	**Baltimore**	Dallas	**16–13**	Miami
IV	1969	**Kansas City**	Minnesota	**23–7**	New Orleans
III	1968	**NY Jets**	Baltimore	**16–7**	Miami
II	1967	**Green Bay**	Oakland	**33–14**	Miami
I	1966	**Green Bay**	Kansas City	**35–10**	Los Angeles

COLLEGE FOOTBALL

A CRIMSON TIDE . . . OF GATORADE!
Alabama players splash head coach Nick Saban with the traditional winner's bath. The team had just defeated Clemson 45–40 to win its 10th national championship and give Saban his fifth title.

Good Timing!

There's an old saying you might have heard before: "Timing is everything." It means that *when* something happens can be as important as *what* happens. That was the story for several big college programs in 2015.

It was the second year of the College Football Playoff, which replaced the Bowl Championship Series. At the end of the regular season, four teams earned a chance at the national title. Rankings were made beginning in early November. Teams moved up and down the list as wins and losses piled up. In the end, the committee chose the "final four." Losing just one game might doom most teams' hopes, but it soon became clear that *when* a team lost was almost as important as *what* team they lost to!

Losing early in the season didn't doom

2015 TOP 10
ASSOCIATED PRESS
1. **Alabama**
2. **Clemson**
3. **Stanford**
4. **Ohio State**
5. **Oklahoma**
6. **Michigan State**
7. **TCU**
8. **Houston**
9. **Iowa**
10. **Mississippi**

a team's chances. However, losing late in the season . . . well, that was another story.

The opening weekend had one of the biggest shocks. Stanford was considered a national-title contender but lost to unranked Northwestern. Down South, Alabama was stunned by an early-season upset loss to Mississippi. Fortunately for the Crimson Tide, however, the Ole Miss defeat came

A late-season loss to Baylor doomed Oklahoma State's chances.

in September. Alabama didn't lose another game the rest of the year.

On the other side of the coin, the Baylor Bears were 8-0 and crushing opponents. But they hit a speed bump on November 14, when they lost 44–34 to Oklahoma. Then the Bears knocked off previously undefeated Oklahoma State the next week, and both those schools finished outside the top four.

Ohio State was the defending national champion and seemed destined for a playoff position. But in late November, the Buckeyes fell to Michigan State, 17–14. Clemson was the only major team to cruise through the regular season without a defeat.

The College Football Playoff makes things very tight from the first weekend to the last. But as Alabama showed in 2015, losing early is not necessarily the end of a national-title chase. Losing late in the season, however, can be a crushing blow.

AWARD WINNERS

HEISMAN TROPHY (BEST PLAYER)
MAXWELL AWARD (PLAYER OF THE YEAR)
WALTER CAMP TROPHY (PLAYER OF THE YEAR)
DOAK WALKER AWARD (RUNNING BACK)
Derrick Henry/ALABAMA ▶

DAVEY O'BRIEN AWARD (QUARTERBACK)
Deshaun Watson/CLEMSON

JOHNNY UNITAS GOLDEN ARM (SENIOR QB)
Connor Cook/MICHIGAN STATE

BILETNIKOFF AWARD (WIDE RECEIVER)
Corey Coleman/BAYLOR

JOHN MACKEY AWARD (TIGHT END)
Hunter Henry/ARKANSAS

OUTLAND TROPHY (INTERIOR LINEMAN)
Joshua Garnett/STANFORD

CHUCK BEDNARIK AWARD (DEFENSIVE PLAYER)
Tyler Matakevich/TEMPLE

BUTKUS AWARD (LINEBACKER)
Jaylon Smith/NOTRE DAME

SEASON HIGHLIGHTS

September

➜ Start With a Bang: BYU got the season off to a stunning start. The Cougars shocked Nebraska 33–28 with a 42-yard touchdown pass on the final play. **Mitch Mathews** came down with the ball while surrounded by three Cornhuskers to spoil the first game for new Cornhuskers' coach **Mike Riley**.

➜ It's About Time: Temple and Penn State played each other 31 times from 1952 through 2014—and Penn State won every time. In 2015, however, Temple broke the streak, upsetting the visiting Nittany Lions 27–10. It was only the Owls' fourth victory in 44 all-time meetings against Penn State (including one game that ended in a tie).

➜ Close but No Cigar: Jacksonville State, a Football Championship Subdivision school, almost had the upset of the year when it took sixth-ranked Auburn to overtime. But the Tigers scored first in the extra session to seal a 27–20 win.

➜ Here's a Tip: No. 3 TCU barely survived against Texas Tech, 55–52. With 52 points against the Horned Frogs' tough defense, the Red Raiders should have had enough to win. But with 23 seconds left, TCU scored on a tipped pass that **Aaron Green** caught at the back of the end zone for the winning score.

➜ Pac-12 Surprise: Oregon has been the story of the Pac-12 in recent years, led by its high-scoring offense and great home record. But on September 26, Utah rolled

Fournette had a big opening month.

into Autzen Stadium (Oregon's home) and crushed the Ducks. Utah used its own high-powered "O" to win 62–20.

➜ Whew!: That's what Florida fans were thinking as they watched Tennessee kicker **Aaron Medley** miss twice from 55 yards with three seconds left. (The first miss came just as Florida called time out.) The Gators had taken the lead on a 63-yard touchdown pass with 1:26 left and won 28–27.

➜ Heisman Hopeful?: LSU running back **Leonard Fournette** put up Heisman-worthy numbers in his team's 34–24 win over Syracuse. The sophomore star ran for 244 yards and scored twice. He had 631 yards and 8 touchdowns in three games in September!

SEASON HIGHLIGHTS
October

➔ **Nice Story:** Although he is blind in one eye and has only a little vision in his other, **Aaron Golub** served as a reserve long snapper for Tulane in 2015. In the team's win over Central Florida, Golub came in to execute a perfect long snap on an extra point!

➔ **No Miracle for the Irish:** No. 6 Notre Dame and No. 12 Clemson faced off in the biggest game of October 3. Clemson got off to a hot start, leading 21–3 entering the fourth quarter. Notre Dame rallied in the second half and scored with seven seconds left but still trailed by two. Clemson rose up to stop the two-point conversion try and left with a hard-earned 24–22 win.

➔ **The Eyes of Texas:** Mighty Texas struggled in the early part of the season. The Longhorns needed a big result in their annual rivalry game against Oklahoma, and they got it. They carried head coach **Charlie Strong** off the field after they upset the No. 10 Sooners 24–17.

➔ **Bad Endings:** In the lowest-scoring game of the season, Wake Forest beat Boston College 3–0. The Eagles had a chance to win but could not get off a final play from the 1-yard line in the final seconds. . . . Rutgers trailed by seven points and had one more shot at the end zone near the end of its game against Michigan State. But quarterback **Chris Laviano** forgot what down

it was and spiked the ball—on fourth down. That let the Spartans hold on to win 31–24.

➔ **Bruins See Red:** Stanford did not act like a nice host when UCLA came to visit. The Cardinal crushed the Bruins 56–35. Stanford's **Christian McCaffrey** set a school record with 243 yards rushing. **Francis Owusu** made one of the best catches of the year, reaching behind a defender to catch a touchdown pass without seeing the ball!

➔ **Two Times Four:** A pair of big games needed four overtimes to decide the winners. Duke tacked on a two-point conversion after scoring a touchdown in the fourth overtime to edge Virginia Tech 45–43. Arkansas scored to go ahead of Auburn 54–46, then held the Tigers out of the end zone to seal the win.

Catch of the year? Owusu caught a TD and a defender!

SEASON HIGHLIGHTS
November

➔ **Sad Saturday:** On the first Saturday of November, four undefeated teams each lost for the first time. No. 2 LSU lost to Alabama, while No. 7 Michigan State, No. 8 TCU, and No. 13 Memphis each lost as well. Michigan State's loss was especially tough. The Spartans fell 39–38 to Nebraska on a 30-yard touchdown pass with just 17 seconds left.

➔ **Hog Shocker:** Arkansas stunned Mississippi in overtime in large part because of a desperation lateral play that gained a key first down on 4th and 25. After scoring a touchdown a moment later, the Razorbacks went for two but didn't make it. However, a penalty on Mississippi gave them another shot. Arkansas made it the second time and won 53–52.

➔ **Western Disaster:** The only two teams out West with a good shot at the playoff saw their chances dim on November 14. Utah was upset by Arizona 37–30. The Wildcats won in the second overtime when backup quarterback **Jerrard Randall** threw his only completed pass of the night. Stanford was ranked No. 7 but lost to unranked Oregon 38–36 at home. The Cardinal had a chance to tie the game on a two-point conversion but couldn't make it work.

➔ **"The Game":** When you're Harvard and Yale and you've played each other 132 times, you get to call your annual contest by that cool name. Harvard has had the hot hand lately. Its 38–19 win this year was its ninth straight, the longest winning streak since the rivalry began back in 1875!

➔ **Playoff Shakeup:** On the final weekend in November, the College Football Playoff was shaken up. First, on Friday, high-flying Baylor was shocked in double overtime by TCU, which won 28–21 in a sloppy game played in the rain. Then, on Saturday night, No. 9 Stanford beat No. 6 Notre Dame 38–36 on a late field goal. The Cardinal had to make the final drive in fewer than 30 seconds to set up **Conrad Ukropina's** 45-yard kick. On the same day, Oklahoma punched its ticket for the playoff with a 58–23 stomping of Oklahoma State.

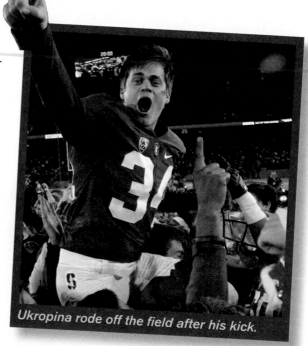

Ukropina rode off the field after his kick.

December

THE CHAMPIONSHIP GAMES

ACC Clemson wrapped up an undefeated regular season with a 45–37 victory over North Carolina. Tigers quarterback **Deshaun Watson** passed for 3 touchdowns and ran for 2 more to lead the way. The Tigers had to survive two late onside kicks while protecting their lead. The win assured Clemson the No. 1 seed in the College Football Playoff.

Big Ten The winner of this game was almost certainly going to make the College Football Playoff. Both teams played great defense. Michigan State managed only field goals until the last minute. Undefeated Iowa held a 13–9 lead, but then the Spartans put together a 22-play drive. With 27 seconds left, Michigan State freshman **L. J. Scott** powered toward the end zone and reached the ball across to score. The 16–13 come-from-behind win earned the Spartans a spot in the playoff.

SEC When you've got a defense like Alabama's and a running back like **Derrick Henry**, you have what you need to win. The Crimson Tide became the first team since Tennessee

Scott stretched for a TD that put Michigan State in the playoff.

in 1998 to win consecutive SEC titles with a 29–15 victory over Florida. Henry set the pace by carrying the ball 44 times for 189 yards and a touchdown. Alabama earned a chance to return to the College Football Playoff, which it lost the previous year.

Pac-12 In the battle for a spot in the Rose Bowl, Stanford repeated an early-season victory over USC. Amazing running back **Christian McCaffrey** piled up 461 yards rushing, receiving, and returning kicks. He even threw a touchdown pass to quarterback **Kevin Hogan**! Stanford won easily, 41–22.

2015 Playoffs

SEMIFINAL 1: ORANGE BOWL

Clemson 37
Oklahoma 17

The Sooners averaged 52 points per game in the second half of the season. Clemson's defense didn't care. After trailing 17–16 at halftime, the Tigers shut down Oklahoma over the final two periods. Clemson quarterback **Deshaun Watson** threw for a touchdown and ran for another, while **Wayne Gallman** ran for a pair of touchdowns. Clemson even set up its first touchdown with a 31-yard pass on a fake punt. The Tigers also picked off two passes while holding OU's rushing attack to 67 yards.

Gallman's running powered Clemson to a big win.

SEMIFINAL 2: COTTON BOWL

Alabama 38
Michigan State 0

When the No. 2 and No. 3 teams in the country meet up for a shot at the title, you don't expect a blowout. But that's what Alabama delivered to Michigan State. Alabama's **Derrick Henry** scored a pair of touchdowns on the ground, while quarterback **Jake Coker** passed for 2 TDs, both to freshman receiver **Calvin Ridley**. 'Bama even scored on a punt return. It was a total domination of a very good team.

4,000/1,000

Clemson's **Deshaun Watson** became the first player in college history to pass for more than 4,000 yards (4,104) and run for more than 1,000 yards (1,105) in the same season.

2015 Championship

Alabama 45, Clemson 40

Well, you wouldn't call it a defensive struggle! With a second-half surge—and two big plays on special teams—Alabama won the national title. It was the fifth for head coach **Nick Saban** (including one at LSU).

Clemson got off to a hot start, leading 14–7 at the end of the first quarter as quarterback **Deshaun Watson** threw 2 of his 4 touchdowns. Alabama tied the score on **Derrick Henry's** 1-yard touchdown run. Earlier, Henry had scored on a 50-yard run; he ended the day with 3 rushing TDs.

The two teams traded scores until it was tied again at 24–24 in the fourth quarter. That's when 'Bama pulled off the surprise of the day. Saban ordered an onside "chip" kick. **Marlon Humphrey** caught it on the fly, and Alabama kept the ball. Moments later, tight end **O. J. Howard** hauled in a 51-yard touchdown pass from **Jake Coker**. Alabama's special teams soon struck again. **Kenyan Drake** returned the kickoff 95 yards for a back-breaking score. Clemson rallied late, but Alabama was the champion.

Howard was a surprise star.

TWO TROPHIES

Here's a list of the Heisman Trophy winners who also earned a national championship in the same season.

YEAR	PLAYER, POS.	SCHOOL	YEAR	PLAYER, POS.	SCHOOL
2015	Derrick Henry, RB	ALABAMA	1976	Tony Dorsett, RB	PITTSBURGH
2013	Jameis Winston, QB	FLORIDA STATE	1949	Leon Hart, End	NOTRE DAME
2010	Cam Newton, QB	AUBURN	1947	Johnny Lujack, QB	NOTRE DAME
2009	Mark Ingram, RB	ALABAMA	1945	Doc Blanchard, RB	ARMY
2004	Matt Leinart, QB	USC	1943	Angelo Bertelli, QB	NOTRE DAME
1997	Charles Woodson, CB	MICHIGAN	1941	Bruce Smith, RB	MINNESOTA
1996	Danny Wuerffel, QB	FLORIDA	1938	Davey O'Brien, QB	TCU
1993	Charlie Ward, QB	FLORIDA STATE			

News and Notes

Look for Goff in the NFL in 2016!

Bowl Bash!

The playoffs were the biggest bowl games of the year, but the rest of the bowls offered plenty of highlights for fans, too. After all, with 40 bowls, you'd expect that some would be pretty awesome! Here are some great memories (for the winners, that is).

◆ **Six for Six:** California QB **Jared Goff** played his final game for the Golden Bears. Goff, who became the top pick in the 2016 NFL Draft, put on a show as Cal beat Air Force 55–36 in the Armed Forces Bowl. He threw 6 touchdown passes, one shy of a bowl record.

◆ **Classic Comeback:** TCU trailed Oregon 31–0 at halftime in the Alamo Bowl. But instead of folding, the Horned Frogs staged a historic comeback. Backup quarterback **Bram Kohlhausen** led his team to the game-tying field goal as time ran out. In the third overtime, his touchdown run gave TCU a 47–41 win.

◆ **Defensive Vacation:** West Virginia and Arizona State piled up 1,196 total yards in the Cactus Bowl. WVU ended up on top 43–42. **Skyler Howard** threw a TD pass to **David Sills** with 2:19 left, and the extra point was the winning margin for the Mountaineers.

Can't Beat the Bison

While the top division's College Football Playoff gets all the headlines, there's excitement at another level, too. That level, known as the Football Championship Series (FCS), is made up of smaller schools. In 2015, North Dakota State won its fifth consecutive FCS championship, defeating Jacksonville State in the final. No football team at any NCAA level has ever matched such a streak!

Fantastic Finishes

Several 2015 games ended on amazing, nail-biting, thrilling plays. Here's a look at some of the most memorable:

◆ **Michigan State 27, Michigan 23** The Wolverines led at home and needed only to punt the ball away to seal a win over the rival Spartans. However, punter **Blake O'Neill** fumbled the snap. It bounced to Michigan State's **Jalen Watts-Jackson**, who stunned the crowd by returning the ball 38 yards for the winning score as time ran out.

◆ **Michigan State 17, Ohio State 14** A month later, the Spartans did it again. After a solid running game set him up,

Michigan State's **Michael Geiger** hit a final-play, 41-yard field goal for the upset victory over the defending national champs.

◆ **Georgia Tech 22, Florida State 16**
With the game tied, ninth-ranked FSU had a chance to escape with a victory. The Seminoles lined up for a game-winning field goal try . . . but it was blocked! Georgia Tech's **Lance Austin** returned the ball 78 yards for a touchdown as time ran out.

◆ **Miami (FL) 30, Duke 27**
"Just keep playing, just keep playing!" That's what Miami coaches must have told their players on the kickoff return that would end this game. Duke had to kick off after its go-ahead score with six seconds left. Miami's players did what they were told. They lateraled the ball eight times. **Corn Elder** snagged the last one and ran 91 yards for the final touchdown.

Reynolds heads for a touchdown splashdown!

The New TD King

Keenan Reynolds will be very busy the next few years. The Navy quarterback hopes to wear both a football uniform and his US Navy officer's gear. In the Military Bowl, his final college game, he set a new NCAA career touchdown record. His 88 scores over four years also included a record 77 rushing touchdowns.

McCaffrey's Busy Season

Christian McCaffrey, Stanford's Mr. Everything, set a new NCAA record for all-purpose yards in 2015. He also scored 15 total TDs. Here's how his amazing season broke down (and this doesn't include his 2 pass completions for 39 yards and 2 touchdowns).

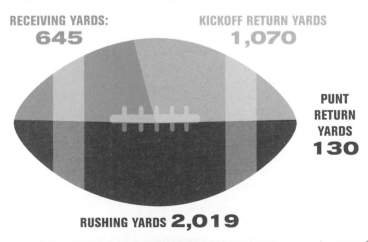

RECEIVING YARDS: **645**

KICKOFF RETURN YARDS **1,070**

PUNT RETURN YARDS **130**

RUSHING YARDS **2,019**

We're No. 1!

These are the teams that have finished at the top of the Associated Press's final rankings since the poll was first introduced in 1936.

SEASON	TEAM	RECORD	SEASON	TEAM	RECORD
2015	Alabama	14-1	1975	Oklahoma	11-1
2014	Ohio State	14-1	1974	Oklahoma	11-0
2013	Florida State	14-0	1973	Notre Dame	11-0
2012	Alabama	13-1	1972	USC	12-0
2011	Alabama	12-1	1971	Nebraska	13-0
2010	Auburn	14-0	1970	Nebraska	11-0-1
2009	Alabama	14-0	1969	Texas	11-0
2008	Florida	13-1	1968	Ohio State	10-0
2007	LSU	12-2	1967	USC	10-1
2006	Florida	13-1	1966	Notre Dame	9-0-1
2005	Texas	13-0	1965	Alabama	9-1-1
2004	USC	13-0	1964	Alabama	10-1
2003	USC	12-1	1963	Texas	11-0
2002	Ohio State	14-0	1962	USC	11-0
2001	Miami (FL)	12-0	1961	Alabama	11-0
2000	Oklahoma	13-0	1960	Minnesota	8-2
1999	Florida State	12-0	1959	Syracuse	11-0
1998	Tennessee	13-0	1958	LSU	11-0
1997	Michigan	12-0	1957	Auburn	10-0
1996	Florida	12-1	1956	Oklahoma	10-0
1995	Nebraska	12-0	1955	Oklahoma	11-0
1994	Nebraska	13-0	1954	Ohio State	10-0
1993	Florida State	12-1	1953	Maryland	10-1
1992	Alabama	13-0	1952	Michigan State	9-0
1991	Miami (FL)	12-0	1951	Tennessee	10-1
1990	Colorado	11-1-1	1950	Oklahoma	10-1
1989	Miami (FL)	11-1	1949	Notre Dame	10-0
1988	Notre Dame	12-0	1948	Michigan	9-0
1987	Miami (FL)	12-0	1947	Notre Dame	9-0
1986	Penn State	12-0	1946	Notre Dame	8-0-1
1985	Oklahoma	11-1	1945	Army	9-0
1984	Brigham Young	13-0	1944	Army	9-0
1983	Miami (FL)	11-1	1943	Notre Dame	9-1
1982	Penn State	11-1	1942	Ohio State	9-1
1981	Clemson	12-0	1941	Minnesota	8-0
1980	Georgia	12-0	1940	Minnesota	8-0
1979	Alabama	12-0	1939	Texas A&M	11-0
1978	Alabama	11-1	1938	Texas Christian	11-0
1977	Notre Dame	11-1	1937	Pittsburgh	9-0-1
1976	Pittsburgh	12-0	1936	Minnesota	7-1

NATIONAL CHAMPIONSHIP GAMES

Until the 2014 season, there was no national championship playoff system at the highest level of college football. From 1998 to 2013, the NCAA ran the Bowl Championship Series, which used computers and polls to come up with a final game that pitted the No. 1 team against the No. 2 team. The new system, called the College Football Playoff, has a panel of experts that sets up a pair of semifinal games to determine which teams play for the national title. Here are the results of BCS and College Football Playoff finals since 2000.

SEASON	TEAMS AND SCORE	SITE
2015	Alabama 45, Clemson 40	GLENDALE, AZ
2014	Ohio State 42, Oregon 20	ARLINGTON, TX
2013	Florida State 34, Auburn 31	PASADENA, CA
2012	Alabama 42, Notre Dame 14	MIAMI, FL
2011	Alabama 21, LSU 0	NEW ORLEANS, LA
2010	Auburn 22, Oregon 19	GLENDALE, AZ
2009	Alabama 37, Texas 21	PASADENA, CA
2008	Florida 24, Oklahoma 14	MIAMI, FL
2007	LSU 38, Ohio State 24	NEW ORLEANS, LA
2006	Florida 41, Ohio State 14	GLENDALE, AZ
2005	Texas 41, USC 38	PASADENA, CA
2004	USC 55, Oklahoma 19	MIAMI, FL
2003	LSU 21, Oklahoma 14	NEW ORLEANS, LA
2002	Ohio State 31, Miami (FL) 24 (2 OT)	TEMPE, AZ
2001	Miami (FL) 37, Nebraska 14	PASADENA, CA
2000	Oklahoma 13, Florida State 2	MIAMI, FL

MLB

ROYAL WELCOME
Royals catcher Salvador Perez, the 2016 World Series MVP, grabbed closer Wade Davis to start the celebration. Kansas City had just won its first World Series since 1985, capping an exciting postseason. Read all about it starting on page 70 .

Blue October!

Every new Major League Baseball season creates another chance for a team to get back on track. In 2015, several teams that had not seen much success for a while suddenly found themselves just a few steps from the World Series.

In the National League, the New York Mets made the playoffs for the first time since 2006 while winning only their second division title since 1988! The Mets used power pitching to move into contention, then added slugger **Yoenis Cespedes** in midseason. He jump-started the offense and sent the Mets into October.

In Chicago, Cubs fans got to enjoy the playoffs for the first time since 2008. Led by rookie slugger **Kris Bryant** and pitcher **Jake Arrieta**, Chicago earned a wild-card spot.

The American League playoff teams included a trio of surprise entries. The last time the Toronto Blue Jays were in the playoffs, they won the World Series . . . the *1993* World

Series! In 2015, Toronto won the AL East for the first time since that championship season. **Jose "Joey Bats" Bautista**, **Edwin Encarnacion**, and league MVP **Josh Donaldson** made the Blue Jays an offensive powerhouse. They scored 891 runs to lead the majors (127 runs more than the second-place New York Yankees).

A pair of Texas teams crashed the postseason party. The Texas Rangers lost 95 games in 2014. Then, at 2015 spring training, they lost ace pitcher **Yu Darvish** for the season to injury. No worries! The Rangers combined solid pitching with the bats of **Prince Fielder** and **Adrian Beltre** to win the AL West for the first time since they made the World Series in 2011. Meanwhile, the Houston Astros were everyone's favorite to succeed—in 2016! A crop of young stars came together a year early to lead the AL West most of the summer. A September swoon left Houston in a battle for the final wild-card spot. The 'Stros and the Los Angeles Angels took it to the final Sunday, when the Rangers did their cross-state rivals a favor by defeating the Halos.

Also in the West, the Los Angeles Dodgers made it to the NL

Adding Cespedes in midseason turned the Mets into contenders.

687

That's **Alex Rodriguez's** career homer total through 2015, putting him fourth all-time behind only **Barry Bonds**, **Hank Aaron**, and **Babe Ruth**. Nice company!

Jose Altuve's gritty play inspired the Astros.

playoffs for the third consecutive year. For a club that has had as much success as the Dodgers, it was a surprise to learn it was the first time they had ever made it three in a row.

Of course, for some teams it was old hat. The St. Louis Cardinals became the first team since 2011 to win 100 games. They also won the NL Central for the ninth time since 2000.

In the AL, the Kansas City Royals, the 2014 World Series runners-up, stayed on top of the league. They had the AL's best record and cruised to the Central title. After two years away, the Yankees returned to the postseason. They have not missed three straight postseasons since 1994!

After 162 games each, the 30 MLB teams turned into the Titanic 10. Then the final two clubs made it a Blue October. Let the postseason begin . . . and read all about it on the following pages!

2015 FINAL STANDINGS

(*Playoff teams)

AL EAST		AL CENTRAL		AL WEST	
Blue Jays*	93–69	Royals*	95–67	Rangers*	88–74
Yankees*	87–75	Twins	83–79	Astros*	86–76
Orioles	81–81	Indians	81–80	Angels	85–77
Rays	80–82	White Sox	76–86	Mariners	76–86
Red Sox	78–84	Tigers	74–87	Athletics	68–94

NL EAST		NL CENTRAL		NL WEST	
Mets*	90–72	Cardinals*	100–62	Dodgers*	92–70
Nationals	83–79	Pirates*	98–64	Giants	84–78
Marlins	71–91	Cubs*	97–65	Diamondbacks	79–83
Braves	67–95	Brewers	68–94	Padres	74–88
Phillies	63–99	Reds	64–98	Rockies	68–94

The Playoffs!

DIVISION SERIES

AMERICAN LEAGUE

Blue Jays 3, Rangers 2

The Rangers surprised the powerful Blue Jays by winning the first two games in Toronto. Then the Jays turned the tables, winning a pair in Texas. That set things up for a wild-and-crazy Game 5. In the seventh inning, Toronto catcher **Russell Martin**'s return throw to the pitcher hit the bat of the Texas hitter. The ball rolled away as the go-ahead run scored! Many longtime fans could not remember seeing another play like it. In the bottom of the inning, Texas committed errors on three consecutive plays. **Josh Donaldson** drove in the tying run, then **Jose Bautista** crushed a three-run homer. The Jays won the game 6–3 and the series.

Royals 3, Astros 2

After heading into Game 4 needing one game to win and then leading 6–2 in that game, Houston thought it had the series sewn up. Not so fast. Kansas City roared back late in the game to win 9–6 and force a Game 5. In front of their home fans, the Royals did not disappoint. **Johnny Cueto** allowed only two hits in eight innings, **Kendrys Morales** had a three-run homer, and the Royals won 7–2.

Bautista's bash sent Toronto into the next round of the playoffs.

Dexter Fowler (right) had one of six homers for the Cubs.

NATIONAL LEAGUE

Cubs 3, Cardinals 1

For the first time in Wrigley Field's 101-year history, its fans saw the home team wrap up a postseason series win. Chicago used the long ball to send the 100-win Cardinals home in four games. After splitting the first two games in St. Louis, the Cubs won a pair at Wrigley. The highlight was their 8–6 win in Game 3. Each of the Cubs' first six batters in the lineup hit a home run in the game, setting an MLB postseason record.

Mets 3, Dodgers 2

After the Mets won Game 1, the Dodgers tied the series in Game 2. In that game, Los Angeles' **Chase Utley** slid hard into New York shortstop **Ruben Tejada**, who suffered a broken leg. Fired up, the Mets won Game 3 with a mighty offensive explosion, setting a team postseason record for runs in their 13–7 win. In Game 4, the Dodgers relied on ace **Clayton Kershaw**, who threw seven innings of one run ball in a 3–1 victory. In Game 5, **Daniel Murphy**'s home run off **Zack Greinke** was the difference as the Mets won 3–2 in Los Angeles.

WILD CARDS!

To reach the Division Series, the Astros sent the once-mighty New York Yankees home early. Houston won the American League Wild-Card Playoff game with a 3–0 shutout of the Yanks on the road. In the National League, the teams with the second-best (Pittsburgh Pirates) and third-best (Chicago Cubs) records during the regular season faced off. Some fans thought that was unfair, but those were the rules! The Cubs won in Pittsburgh, 4–0.

Championship Series

American League
Royals 4, Blue Jays 2

The Royals got a jump on the favored Blue Jays by winning a pair of games in Kansas City. Royals pitcher **Edinson Volquez** bottled up Toronto's big-hitting lineup in Game 1. In Game 2, the Royals surprised Toronto ace **David Price** with five runs in the seventh to come from behind. Back in Toronto, the Blue Jays' bats woke up, and they won two of three games. However, the Royals put on a power display of their own and won Game 4, 14–2. In Kansas City, Game 6 was tied 3–3 in the eighth. Then the Royals' **Lorenzo Cain** scored from first base on a single by **Eric Hosmer** with what proved to be the winning run. The Royals made it back-to-back AL titles and hoped for their first Series win since 1985.

ALCS MVP: Alcides Escobar, Kansas City

National League
Mets 4, Cubs 0

It was all about the Murph. Mets second baseman **Daniel Murphy** had home runs in each of the first two games. The Mets won both games, helped by great pitching from **Matt Harvey** and **Noah Syndergaard**. In Chicago, Murph kept mashing. He ended up with homers in each of the four NLCS games. Along with a pair of home runs in the Division Series, he set a new record by going yard in six consecutive postseason games. The Mets swept into their first World Series since 2000.

NLCS MVP: Daniel Murphy, New York

Cain's mad dash for home surprised catcher Russell Martin and the Blue Jays.

2015 World Series

One thing was for sure: The winner of this World Series would have waited a *loooong* time. The Mets had not been the best in baseball since 1986. The Royals last were champs in 1985. In the end, Kansas City's comeback ability, all-around balance, and relentless play made the difference.

GAME 1:
Royals 5, Mets 4

This was an instant classic. At 14 innings, it tied for the longest World Series game! Kansas City's **Alcides Escobar** hit the first pitch in the bottom of the first inning for an inside-the-park home run, the first in the World Series since 1929! With the Mets ahead in the ninth, **Alex Gordon** crushed a dramatic homer to tie the game. **Chris Young** pitched three hitless extra innings before the Royals won in the 14th on **Eric Hosmer's** sac fly.

GAME 2:
Royals 7, Mets 1

Pitcher **Johnny Cueto** was lights-out. He held the Mets to two hits and threw the first complete-game win by an AL World Series pitcher in 24 years!

GAME 3: Mets 9, Royals 3

New York loved being home, as **Noah Syndergaard** threw six strong innings and **David Wright** had four RBI. **Curtis Granderson** added a two-run homer. Here's a bit of trivia: **Raul Mondesi** pinch-hit for the Royals in the fifth inning. He became the first player ever to make his Major League debut in a World Series game! (He struck out.)

Cueto was a Royals ace.

GAME 4:
Royals 5, Mets 3

Kansas City's Comeback Kids did it again. Trailing by a run entering the eighth inning, the Royals took advantage of an error by **Daniel Murphy** to help them score three times. The Mets could not recover, and the Royals went ahead three games to one. Not even two homers by rookie **Michael Conforto** could save the Mets.

GAME 5:
Royals 7, Mets 2

For the record seventh time in this postseason, the Royals trailed by at least two runs . . . and came back to win. This time, they waited until the ninth inning for their heroics. Mets pitcher **Matt Harvey** bottled up the Royals for eight innings. Harvey talked manager **Terry Collins** into letting him pitch the ninth. After giving up a walk and an RBI double, Harvey was out. The Royals tied the score when Hosmer made a daring base-running move, scoring from third on a groundout. The game went to extra innings. Kansas City scored five runs in the 12th inning to clinch the game and their first World Series championship in 30 years.

WS MVP: Salvador Perez, Kansas City

Award Winners

MOST VALUABLE PLAYER

AL: **Josh Donaldson**
BLUE JAYS

NL: **Bryce Harper**
NATIONALS

CY YOUNG AWARD

AL: **Dallas Keuchel**
ASTROS

NL: **Jake Arrieta**
CUBS

ROOKIE OF THE YEAR

AL: **Carlos Correa**
ASTROS

NL: **Kris Bryant**
CUBS

MANAGER OF THE YEAR

AL: **Jeff Banister**
RANGERS

NL: **Joe Maddon**
CUBS

ROBERTO CLEMENTE AWARD
(FOR COMMUNITY SERVICE)

Andrew McCutchen
PIRATES

Keuchel was the AL's top pitcher.

5

Not a big number, but a big beard! That's the approximate length in inches of **Dallas Keuchel's** beard. He grew it in 2014 and has been an ace ever since.

Stat Champs

AL Hitting Leaders

47 HOME RUNS
Chris Davis, Orioles

123 RBI
Josh Donaldson, Blue Jays

.338 BATTING AVERAGE
Miguel Cabrera, Tigers

38 STOLEN BASES
200 HITS
Jose Altuve, Astros

NL Hitting Leaders

42 HOME RUNS
Nolan Arenado, Rockies
Bryce Harper, Nationals

130 RBI
Nolan Arenado, Rockies

.333 BATTING AVERAGE
58 STOLEN BASES
205 HITS
Dee Gordon, Marlins

With 123 RBI, Donaldson was clutch for Toronto.

AL Pitching Leaders

20 WINS
Dallas Keuchel, Astros

41 SAVES
Brad Boxberger, Rays

2.45 ERA
David Price, Blue Jays

274 STRIKEOUTS
Chris Sale, White Sox

NL Pitching Leaders

22 WINS
Jake Arrieta, Cubs

51 SAVES
Mark Melancon, Pirates

1.66 ERA
Zack Greinke, Dodgers

301 STRIKEOUTS
Clayton Kershaw, Dodgers

Around the Bases 2015

Sensational Scherzer: In the final week of the season, Nationals pitcher **Max Scherzer** turned in one of the best pitching performances in baseball history. Scherzer threw his second no-hitter of the regular season–he was the first pitcher since 1973 to do that!–while walking no one. The only base runner came on a sixth-inning error. Plus, Scherzer struck out 17, a record for a no-hit, no-walk game. That also was the most by a Nationals pitcher in any game ever! Max was magic!

Dynamite Dodger Duo!: The Dodgers boasted one of the best pitching combos in the game. In the summer of 2015, **Clayton Kershaw** and **Zack Greinke** dueled to see just who was number one. Greinke went 45 2/3 innings without giving up a run. Kershaw attempted to surpass that feat. He ran off a streak of 37 consecutive scoreless innings that ended in August. Wow! (Trivia time: The top two MLB shutout streaks ever are both by Dodgers–59 innings by **Orel Hershiser** and 58 2/3 by **Don Drysdale**.)

TROUT ON TOP

Mike Trout has led the American League in many stat categories since joining the Angels in 2011. Plus, he was first or second in the MVP voting each year from 2012 to 2015!

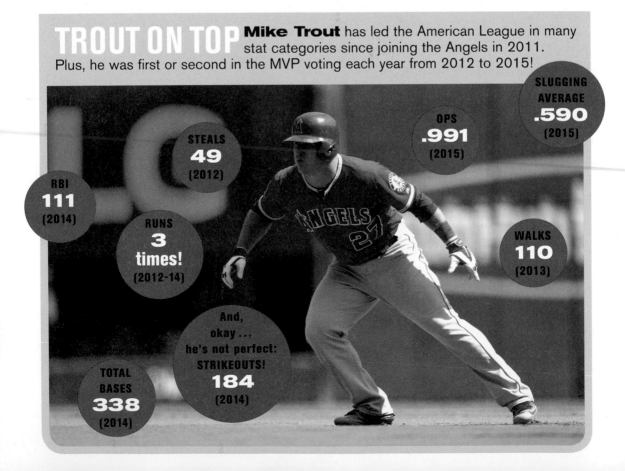

SLUGGING AVERAGE
.590
(2015)

OPS
.991
(2015)

STEALS
49
(2012)

RBI
111
(2014)

RUNS
3
times!
(2012-14)

WALKS
110
(2013)

And, okay ...
he's not perfect:
STRIKEOUTS!
184
(2014)

TOTAL BASES
338
(2014)

Historic Highlights

A few short stops to fill you in on momentous moments:

◄ When the Rangers' **Adrian Beltre** hit for the cycle—a single, double, triple, and home run—in a game in August, he became only the fourth player ever with three cycles in a career. The last: **Babe Herman**, way back in 1933!

✱ Boston didn't make a dent in the standings in 2015. But in August, the Red Sox made a dent in their opponents. They became the first team since 1950 to rack up 15 or more runs and 21 or more hits in back-to-back games. (The last team to do it? That's right: the Red Sox!)

✱ Baseball has been around a long time, so some records really last. One that fell in 2015 was the Chicago White Sox single-season strikeout record. With an American League-leading 274 Ks, **Chris Sale** broke a team record that had stood since 1908!

✱ It's bad enough being no-hit; try doing it twice in 10 days! First, on August 21, Houston's **Mike Fiers** kept the Dodgers hitless. Nine days later, **Jake Arrieta** of the Cubs did the same to the Los Angeles team. It was the first time a team put up a zero in the hits column in that short of a time span since 1923!

Home-Run Heroes: ▶▶▶

A tip of the cap to a pair of sluggers who made news in 2015. **David "Big Papi" Ortiz** gave Red Sox fans a reason to cheer in an otherwise tough season. On September 12, he blasted a pair of homers against the Rays. The second gave him 500 for his career. He joins a club with just 26 other members. In the minor leagues, **Mike Hessman** cracked the 433rd home run of his career, making him the all-time minor-league champ.

One Crowded Scorecard:

In a 16-inning game in September, the Dodgers and Rockies wore out the scorekeeper. Including many rookie call-ups, they combined to use an all-time record 58 players. That included 24 pitchers, another single-game record. Oh, yes, the Rockies won 5–4, if you're keeping score, too!

Around the Bases 2016

What a Story!: Colorado shortstop **Trevor Story** got off to a very hot start. He was the first player since 1900 to have each of his first four career hits be a home run. And he was the first player ever to homer in each of his first three big-league games! Story clubbed 6 homers in the first four games of the season, a Major League first for any player, rookie or not. Watch the Rockies to see if he can keep it up!

A Triple Play First: They've been keeping records of baseball games for more than 115 years. You'd think that just about everything that could have happened . . . had happened. Not so fast. The Chicago White Sox pulled off a triple play against the Texas Rangers that was an all-time first. The first out was a catch in right field. A throw to first base doubled off a runner for the second out. Then a rundown that used three defensive players accounted for the third out. The first-ever play was scored 9-3-2-6-2-5. That's right fielder to first baseman to catcher to shortstop to catcher to third baseman. Whew!

◀◀◀ Awesome Arrieta: The Chicago Cubs began the 2016 season by winning 24 of their first 30 games. That's the best start since Detroit in 1984. (The Tigers went on to win that year's World Series, Cubs fans!) A big part of the Cubs' success was pitcher **Jake Arrieta**. Dating to 2015, the Cubs won 23 consecutive games that he started. The streak, which ended in June, was one of the longest in baseball history. Arrieta himself won 20 consecutive decisions before the Diamondbacks got to him. In April,

2016 Hall of Fame Class

A Fame-ous New Record

In his first year on the ballot, superstar outfielder **Ken Griffey Jr.** was elected to the Baseball Hall of Fame with 99.3 percent of voters choosing him. That was the highest mark in the 80-year history of Hall voting. Griffey slugged 630 homers, won nine Gold Gloves, and was named to 13 All-Star Games. He played 22 seasons, mostly with the Mariners and Reds. Griffey's dad, **Ken**, was also a big-leaguer. In 1990 and 1991, they played together in the Mariners' outfield! Ken Jr. brought a real love of the game to every ballpark he played in.

Mike Catches the Hall

Slugging catcher **Mike Piazza** was also elected to the Hall. Some experts consider Piazza the best-hitting catcher of all time. The 1993 Rookie of the Year, he had a .308 career average and was named to 12 All-Star Games. He starred with the Dodgers and Mets, and helped New York win the National League pennant in 2000. Amazingly, this great player was chosen in the 62nd round (the 1,390th pick overall) of the 1988 MLB Draft. He's the lowest-drafted player ever to climb the Hall-of-Fame ladder.

Arrieta tossed his second career no-hitter, a 16–0 rout of the Reds.

* **Hit King:** Miami's **Ichirō Suzuki** became the 30th player to reach 3,000 hits. Of course, milestones are nothing new for him, since he already had the record for hits by a rookie (201 in 2001) and hits in a season (262 in 2004). He also had 1,278 hits in Japan before joining the Majors. Omedetogozaimasu*, Ichirō! (*Congratulations!)

* **K Crazy!:** **Max Scherzer** of the Washington Nationals pitched what some experts called one of the best games ever thrown in the big leagues. The 2013 Cy Young Award winner became only the fifth pitcher ever to strike out 20 batters in nine innings, as Washington beat Detroit 3–2. His percentage of strikes was the highest among those five pitchers. (Of his 119 pitches, 96 were in the zone.) Max gave up only six hits . . . and no walks!

World Series Winners

YEAR	WINNER	RUNNER-UP	SCORE*	YEAR	WINNER	RUNNER-UP	SCORE*
2015	Kansas City Royals	New York Mets	4-1	1988	Los Angeles Dodgers	Oakland Athletics	4-1
2014	San Francisco Giants	Kansas City Royals	4-3	1987	Minnesota Twins	St. Louis Cardinals	4-3
2013	Boston Red Sox	St. Louis Cardinals	4-2	1986	New York Mets	Boston Red Sox	4-3
2012	San Francisco Giants	Detroit Tigers	4-0	1985	Kansas City Royals	St. Louis Cardinals	4-3
2011	St. Louis Cardinals	Texas Rangers	4-3	1984	Detroit Tigers	San Diego Padres	4-1
2010	San Francisco Giants	Texas Rangers	4-1	1983	Baltimore Orioles	Philadelphia Phillies	4-1
2009	New York Yankees	Philadelphia Phillies	4-2	1982	St. Louis Cardinals	Milwaukee Brewers	4-3
2008	Philadelphia Phillies	Tampa Bay Rays	4-1	1981	Los Angeles Dodgers	New York Yankees	4-2
2007	Boston Red Sox	Colorado Rockies	4-0	1980	Philadelphia Phillies	Kansas City Royals	4-2
2006	St. Louis Cardinals	Detroit Tigers	4-1	1979	Pittsburgh Pirates	Baltimore Orioles	4-3
2005	Chicago White Sox	Houston Astros	4-0	1978	New York Yankees	Los Angeles Dodgers	4-2
2004	Boston Red Sox	St. Louis Cardinals	4-0	1977	New York Yankees	Los Angeles Dodgers	4-2
2003	Florida Marlins	New York Yankees	4-2	1976	Cincinnati Reds	New York Yankees	4-0
2002	Anaheim Angels	San Francisco Giants	4-3	1975	Cincinnati Reds	Boston Red Sox	4-3
2001	Arizona Diamondbacks	New York Yankees	4-3	1974	Oakland Athletics	Los Angeles Dodgers	4-1
2000	New York Yankees	New York Mets	4-1	1973	Oakland Athletics	New York Mets	4-3
1999	New York Yankees	Atlanta Braves	4-0	1972	Oakland Athletics	Cincinnati Reds	4-3
1998	New York Yankees	San Diego Padres	4-0	1971	Pittsburgh Pirates	Baltimore Orioles	4-3
1997	Florida Marlins	Cleveland Indians	4-3	1970	Baltimore Orioles	Cincinnati Reds	4-1
1996	New York Yankees	Atlanta Braves	4-2	1969	New York Mets	Baltimore Orioles	4-1
1995	Atlanta Braves	Cleveland Indians	4-2	1968	Detroit Tigers	St. Louis Cardinals	4-3
1993	Toronto Blue Jays	Philadelphia Phillies	4-2	1967	St. Louis Cardinals	Boston Red Sox	4-3
1992	Toronto Blue Jays	Atlanta Braves	4-2	1966	Baltimore Orioles	Los Angeles Dodgers	4-0
1991	Minnesota Twins	Atlanta Braves	4-3	1965	Los Angeles Dodgers	Minnesota Twins	4-3
1990	Cincinnati Reds	Oakland Athletics	4-0	1964	St. Louis Cardinals	New York Yankees	4-3
1989	Oakland Athletics	San Francisco Giants	4-0	1963	Los Angeles Dodgers	New York Yankees	4-0

* Score is represented in games played.

YEAR	WINNER	RUNNER-UP	SCORE*	YEAR	WINNER	RUNNER-UP	SCORE*
1962	New York Yankees	San Francisco Giants	4-3	1932	New York Yankees	Chicago Cubs	4-0
1961	New York Yankees	Cincinnati Reds	4-1	1931	St. Louis Cardinals	Philadelphia Athletics	4-3
1960	Pittsburgh Pirates	New York Yankees	4-3	1930	Philadelphia Athletics	St. Louis Cardinals	4-2
1959	Los Angeles Dodgers	Chicago White Sox	4-2	1929	Philadelphia Athletics	Chicago Cubs	4-1
1958	New York Yankees	Milwaukee Braves	4-3	1928	New York Yankees	St. Louis Cardinals	4-0
1957	Milwaukee Braves	New York Yankees	4-3	1927	New York Yankees	Pittsburgh Pirates	4-0
1956	New York Yankees	Brooklyn Dodgers	4-3	1926	St. Louis Cardinals	New York Yankees	4-3
1955	Brooklyn Dodgers	New York Yankees	4-3	1925	Pittsburgh Pirates	Washington Senators	4-3
1954	New York Giants	Cleveland Indians	4-0	1924	Washington Senators	New York Giants	4-3
1953	New York Yankees	Brooklyn Dodgers	4-2	1923	New York Yankees	New York Giants	4-2
1052	New York Yankees	Brooklyn Dodgers	4-3	1922	New York Giants	New York Yankees	4-0
1951	New York Yankees	New York Giants	4-2	1921	New York Giants	New York Yankees	5-3
1950	New York Yankees	Philadelphia Phillies	4-0	1920	Cleveland Indians	Brooklyn Robins	5-2
1949	New York Yankees	Brooklyn Dodgers	4-1	1919	Cincinnati Reds	Chicago White Sox	5-3
1948	Cleveland Indians	Boston Braves	4-2	1918	Boston Red Sox	Chicago Cubs	4-2
1947	New York Yankees	Brooklyn Dodgers	4-3	1917	Chicago White Sox	New York Giants	4-2
1946	St. Louis Cardinals	Boston Red Sox	4-3	1916	Boston Red Sox	Brooklyn Robins	4-1
1945	Detroit Tigers	Chicago Cubs	4-3	1915	Boston Red Sox	Philadelphia Phillies	4-1
1944	St. Louis Cardinals	St. Louis Browns	4-2	1914	Boston Braves	Philadelphia Athletics	4-0
1943	New York Yankees	St. Louis Cardinals	4-1	1913	Philadelphia Athletics	New York Giants	4-1
1942	St. Louis Cardinals	New York Yankees	4-1	1912	Boston Red Sox	New York Giants	4-3
1941	New York Yankees	Brooklyn Dodgers	4-1	1911	Philadelphia Athletics	New York Giants	4-2
1940	Cincinnati Reds	Detroit Tigers	4-3	1910	Philadelphia Athletics	Chicago Cubs	4-1
1939	New York Yankees	Cincinnati Reds	4-0	1909	Pittsburgh Pirates	Detroit Tigers	4-3
1938	New York Yankees	Chicago Cubs	4-0	1908	Chicago Cubs	Detroit Tigers	4-1
1937	New York Yankees	New York Giants	4-1	1907	Chicago Cubs	Detroit Tigers	4-0
1936	New York Yankees	New York Giants	4-2	1906	Chicago White Sox	Chicago Cubs	4-2
1935	Detroit Tigers	Chicago Cubs	4-2	1905	New York Giants	Philadelphia Athletics	4-1
1934	St. Louis Cardinals	Detroit Tigers	4-3	1903	Boston Americans	Pittsburgh Pirates	5-3
1933	New York Giants	Washington Senators	4-1				

Note: 1904 not played because NL-champion Giants refused to play; 1994 not played due to MLB work stoppage.

OH . . . MY . . . GOODNESS!
Kris Jenkins secured a spot in basketball history with this dramatic shot. His three-point, buzzer-beating bucket gave Villanova a 77–74 win over North Carolina for the national championship. It capped off what many experts called one of the best final games ever played.

COLLEGE BASKETBALL

Epic Endings

Both the men's and women's college hoops seasons provided fans with historic and memorable endings (see pages 89 and 91), but each took a very different path to get there.

On the men's side, there was no clear No. 1. Several teams had their chance atop the rankings, only to fall victim to upsets. Kansas and Michigan State spent the most time at No. 1, but they had to take turns with Kentucky, North Carolina, Villanova, and Oklahoma.

Maryland, Xavier, and Virginia also made runs near the top of the list, showing the depth of talent across all of college hoops. Defending champion Duke found itself out of the rankings for the first time in years, though the Blue Devils eventually made it back to the top 15.

The NCAA tournament followed the path of the regular season. There were numerous upsets in early rounds— most notably of Michigan State. Kansas entered the tournament ranked No. 1, but no team really set itself apart from the pack . . . until the final shot of the season determined the champion.

On the women's side, there was no question what team was best. The University of Connecticut did not lose a single game. In fact, the Huskies won all 38 of their games by 10 or more points. They completed an amazing stretch in which they won an all-time record 151 games in four seasons, including the current streak of 122 out of 123. Leading the way was **Breanna Stewart**, a three-time All-America selection with an all-around game: shooting, passing, and defending. She was joined by senior stars **Morgan Tuck** and **Moriah Jefferson**. Together, the trio led the way in 2015–16, as they had for three previous seasons.

The big surprise in the women's game was the rise of teams from the West. Stanford was in the mix, as it often has been in recent seasons. But in 2016, Washington and Oregon State also rose to join the national elite. As usual, Baylor, Notre Dame, and South Carolina were among the teams chasing Connecticut, too. But in the end, the Huskies proved to be an unstoppable force, and Stewart went out a big winner.

High-scoring Buddy Hield led Oklahoma to the Final Four.

BIG AWARDS

WOODEN AWARD
Buddy Hield/OKLAHOMA
Breanna Stewart/CONNECTICUT ▶

NAISMITH AWARD
Buddy Hield/OKLAHOMA
Breanna Stewart/CONNECTICUT

AP PLAYER OF THE YEAR
Denzel Valentine/MICHIGAN STATE

AP COACH OF THE YEAR
Bill Self/KANSAS

MEN'S 2015–16 TOP 10
USA Today Coaches Poll
1. Villanova
2. North Carolina
3. Kansas
4. Oklahoma
5. Virginia
6. Oregon
7. Michigan State
8. Miami
9. Indiana
10. Syracuse

WOMEN'S 2015–16 TOP 10
USA Today Coaches Poll
1. Connecticut
2. Oregon State
3. Syracuse
4. Baylor
5. South Carolina
6. Notre Dame
7. Texas
8. Washington
9. Maryland
10. Ohio State

2015–16 Highlights

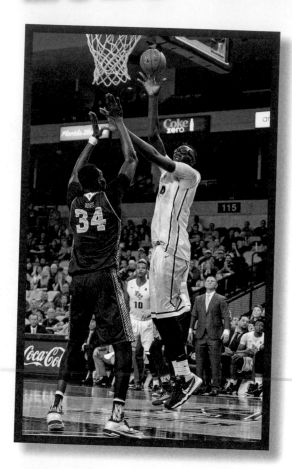

season. Not so for No. 2 Kentucky and No. 5 Duke. They played each other in November! Kentucky won 74–63, but neither team kept its high ranking much longer.

◀◀◀**TALL ORDER:** In November, Tacko Fall of the University of Central Florida and Mamadou Ndiaye (34) of UC Irvine tipped off against each other. Why was it a big deal? Each player is 7 feet, 6 inches tall. They formed the tallest college hoops twosome ever. News stories reported that both players are among the 40 tallest people in the world!

DOWN GOES NO. 1!: In what became a theme this season, as no team held the top spot for more than four consecutive weeks, No. 1 Kentucky was upset by UCLA 87–77 in early December. The win proved a bright spot for the normally solid Bruins, who finished 10th in the Pac-12 and missed the NCAA tournament.

LONG WAY FOR A GAME: To tip off the 2015–16 season, Washington and Texas headed east . . . far east! The teams played the season-opening game in Shanghai, China. That nation has become a hoops hotbed, and its fans enjoyed watching Washington's 77–71 win.

HOT START: Highly ranked teams often start out with weaker opponents to ease into the

HIGH-RANKED ACTION: Although Oklahoma's Buddy Hield scored 46 points— the most put up against a No. 5 or better team in 20 years!—the No. 2 Sooners could not knock off No. 1 Kansas in January. The game was tied at 77–77 after regulation. It took three overtimes for the Jayhawks to win 109–106.

MEN'S NCAA TOURNAMENT
Crazy First Rounds!

The 2016 NCAA men's tournament got off to a crazy start. As usual, millions of fans filled in their brackets, hoping they'd be able to brag at the end. As usual, most of them were shocked by upsets. However, 2016 proved to be even more surprising than usual. A record 10 teams seeded 10 or lower won games in the first round alone. Here are the most amazing results from the first two rounds.

Middle Tennessee State 90, Michigan State 81

No 15th-seeded team had won a first-round game since 2013, and only seven had ever won. That made the Blue Raiders' win the shocker of the first round. In picking tournament brackets, millions of fans had No. 2-seeded Michigan State in the championship game, but the upset busted those brackets.

Stephen F. Austin 70, West Virginia 56

The Lumberjacks were a No. 14 seed, but they played like a No. 1. A powerful defense and 33 points from **Thomas Walkup** combined to give the team from Texas a strong win over the No. 3 Mountaineers.

A shout-out to Middle Tennessee for a big upset!

Hawaii 77, California 66

At No. 4, Cal earned its highest seed ever, but then lost two of its top players before the game. That gave the 13th-seeded Warriors the chance to become the first team from outside the continental US to win a tournament game.

Yale 79, Baylor 75

Yale had not been to the NCAA tournament since 1962. Baylor was a No. 5 seed and expected to go far. But No. 12 Yale pulled off a huge upset, as **Makai Mason** scored a career-best 31 points to lead the Bulldogs.

Arkansas Little Rock 85, Purdue 83 (2 OT)

Josh Hagins was money . . . twice. He nailed a three-pointer to tie the game in the final seconds of regulation play, then banked in a shot to tie it again late in the first overtime. The No. 12 Trojans shocked the No. 5 Boilermakers by winning in the second overtime.

Northern Iowa 75, Texas 72

Seriously? A half-court runner banked in at the buzzer? That's what **Paul Jesperson** did to give the Panthers (who were a No. 11 seed) a shocking win over the Longhorns (a No. 6 seed).

MEN'S NCAA TOURNAMENT
Revealing Regionals

The Pac-12 champion Oregon Ducks (left) stayed hot with a big win over Duke.

EAST: Wisconsin upset Xavier 66–63 to reach the Sweet 16, but the Badgers couldn't top Notre Dame. The Fighting Irish won 61–56. A matchup of basketball powerhouses—North Carolina and Indiana—was high scoring, but not dramatic. The Tar Heels' 101–86 victory set up a North Carolina-Notre Dame regional final. The Tar Heels won 88–74 to reach the Final Four for the 19th time.

SOUTH: No big surprises here, as higher seeds headed to the Elite Eight. Villanova continued to look impressive, pounding Miami 92–69. Kansas made short work of Maryland, 79–63. In the regional final, Villanova, a No. 2 seed, earned its first Final Four spot since 2009 by defeating a solid Kansas team, a No. 1 seed, 64–59.

MIDWEST: No. 10 Syracuse faced surprising No. 11 Gonzaga. Syracuse held on to win an exciting game, 63–60. The Orange then faced powerful Virginia, a No. 1 seed that rolled through Iowa State 84–71. Syracuse pulled off the shocker of the round by defeating the Cavaliers 68–62. The Orange became the first No. 10 seed to reach a Final Four!

WEST: Oregon sent defending champion Duke home earlier than expected with a solid 82–68 win in the first part of this regional. No. 2-seeded Oklahoma beat No. 3-seeded Texas A&M 77–63. In the final, the West Coast advantage was not enough for the Ducks, who lost to high-scoring **Buddy Hield** and the Sooners 80–68.

MEN'S NCAA TOURNAMENT
Fantastic Final Four!

Villanova 95, Oklahoma 51

When your opponents make more than 7 out of every 10 shots, you're in for a long game. That's what Oklahoma was in for in this semifinal. Villanova's 44-point margin of victory was the most ever in a Final Four game, while its 71.4 shooting percentage was the second best ever. The Wildcats locked up the game with a stunning 25–0 run in the second half to cruise to their first national title game since they won it all in 1985 (when they set the shooting percentage record).

North Carolina 83, Syracuse 66

No. 10 Syracuse was playing out of its league in this semifinal. North Carolina was a No. 1 seed and had spent time at the top of the national rankings in the 2015–16 season. The Orange kept it close for a while, but the Tar Heels pulled away for an easy win, led largely by their high-scoring forwards.

CHAMPIONSHIP GAME

Villanova 77,
North Carolina 74 ▶

What a game! Both teams arrived having cruised through the tournament, and their great play continued in the final. It was a back-and-forth game, with nine lead changes and nine ties. A 10-point lead was the largest by either team; it was that close. North Carolina led at the half, but Villanova used a 7–0 run late in the game to take a 67–57 lead with about

five minutes to play. The Tar Heels never gave up, charging back to pull within 3 points. With time running out, Marcus Paige rose up for a three-pointer, pumped once to avoid a defender, and swished in a game-tying basket with 4.7 seconds left. That was enough time for Villanova. Ryan Arcidiacono, named the Most Outstanding Player of the Final Four, dribbled quickly up the court. "Arch" tossed a pass to Kris Jenkins. In rhythm, Jenkins grabbed the ball and lofted a shot. As it rose through the air, the final buzzer sounded . . . and the ball went in. Villanova players mobbed Jenkins, while North Carolina players could only watch, disappointed at how close they had come.

WOMEN'S NCAA TOURNAMENT
The Early Rounds

Here are some of the highlights (or lowlights, depending on who you root for!) from the early rounds of the 2016 NCAA Women's Basketball Tournament.

12 Over 5 Times 2!:
There was bad news for the Sunshine State in the first round. A pair of No. 12 seeds came up with surprising opening-round wins over Florida schools. South Dakota State shocked Miami 74–71, while Albany beat Florida 61–59. (South Dakota State nearly made it two straight upsets. In the next round, the Jackrabbits led Stanford after three quarters, but the No. 4 Cardinal rallied to win 66–65.)

Um . . . Wow:
Connecticut is certainly dominant. But what they did to Mississippi State in the Sweet 16 was epic. The Huskies won by 60 points! It was by far the biggest margin of victory in a women's regional tournament game. Connecticut led 32–4 after the first quarter. The final score: 98–38.

Here Come the Huskies!:
No, not the ones from Connecticut. The Huskies from Washington were the surprise team of the tournament. After defeating Penn in the first round, they beat No. 2-seeded Maryland 74–65. Then they faced a powerful No. 3 Kentucky team . . . and won 85–72. Fourth-seeded Stanford was the next to fall, 85–76. Washington's Cinderella run ended against Syracuse in the Final Four.

Volunteer Victories:
Tennessee has won eight national titles. But this year's team was not the powerhouse of years past. Did help from the old days send the No. 7 Lady Vols to upsets of second-seeded Arizona State (75–64) and third-seeded Ohio State (78–62)? They fell 89–67 in the regional final to Syracuse, however.

Orange Women!:
While the Syracuse men (see page 88) were shocking fans, the Syracuse women were doing just fine, too, thank you. They reached their regional semifinal to find No. 1-seeded South Carolina waiting for them. But with a great performance from **Alexis Peterson** (26 points), Syracuse posted an 80–72 upset victory, then defeated Tennessee to reach the Final Four for the first time.

Black-clad Washington swarmed over Maryland to pull the upset.

WOMEN'S NCAA TOURNAMENT
Final Four

SYRACUSE 80, WASHINGTON 59

In a battle of Final Four first-timers, Syracuse's tough defense was the difference. Washington's **Talia Walton** set a Final Four record with 8 three-point baskets, but it was not enough. Syracuse's **Brianna Butler** set her own three-point mark, establishing an NCAA single-season best with 128 treys. Syracuse advanced to its first NCAA championship game.

CONNECTICUT 80, OREGON STATE 51

Breanna Stewart was in foul trouble early, but the Huskies showed how deep they were. **Morgan Tuck** scored 16 of her 21 points in the first half, while Stewart contributed 14 in the second half. The Huskies won easily over the Beavers, who were making their first appearance in the Final Four. The 29-point margin was the largest ever in a women's Final Four game.

CHAMPIONSHIP GAME
CONNECTICUT 82, SYRACUSE 51

At 38–0, Connecticut capped its sixth undefeated season. (No other school even has more than one.) The Huskies won their 11th national championship, including their fourth in a row. Longtime coach **Geno Auriemma**

Stewart was the best for the fourth time.

moved past the 10 titles won by UCLA's legendary men's coach **John Wooden** to take over the lead in career NCAA championships. **Breanna Stewart** became the first player ever—man or woman—to win four Most Outstanding Player awards at the Final Four. She had a team-high 24 points in the final, along with 10 rebounds. It was over early (50–23 at the half), though Syracuse gave it the old college try. Trailing 60–27 in the third quarter, Syracuse went on a 16–0 run to make it closer. But then UConn put on the jets again and cruised to yet another remarkable win.

NCAA Champs!

MEN'S DIVISION I

2016 **Villanova**	1998 **Kentucky**	1980 **Louisville**
2015 **Duke**	1997 **Arizona**	1979 **Michigan State**
2014 **Connecticut**	1996 **Kentucky**	1978 **Kentucky**
2013 **Louisville**	1995 **UCLA**	1977 **Marquette**
2012 **Kentucky**	1994 **Arkansas**	1976 **Indiana**
2011 **Connecticut**	1993 **North Carolina**	1975 **UCLA**
2010 **Duke**	1992 **Duke**	1974 **NC State**
2009 **North Carolina**	1991 **Duke**	1973 **UCLA**
2008 **Kansas**	1990 **UNLV**	1972 **UCLA**
2007 **Florida**	1989 **Michigan**	1971 **UCLA**
2006 **Florida**	1988 **Kansas**	1970 **UCLA**
2005 **North Carolina**	1987 **Indiana**	1969 **UCLA**
2004 **Connecticut**	1986 **Louisville**	1968 **UCLA**
2003 **Syracuse**	1985 **Villanova**	1967 **UCLA**
2002 **Maryland**	1984 **Georgetown**	1966 **Texas Western**
2001 **Duke**	1983 **NC State**	1965 **UCLA**
2000 **Michigan State**	1982 **North Carolina**	1964 **UCLA**
1999 **Connecticut**	1981 **Indiana**	1963 **Loyola (Illinois)**

1962 **Cincinnati**	1954 **La Salle**	1946 **Oklahoma A&M**
1961 **Cincinnati**	1953 **Indiana**	1945 **Oklahoma A&M**
1960 **Ohio State**	1952 **Kansas**	1944 **Utah**
1959 **California**	1951 **Kentucky**	1943 **Wyoming**
1958 **Kentucky**	1950 **City Coll. of NY**	1942 **Stanford**
1957 **North Carolina**	1949 **Kentucky**	1941 **Wisconsin**
1956 **San Francisco**	1948 **Kentucky**	1940 **Indiana**
1955 **San Francisco**	1947 **Holy Cross**	1939 **Oregon**

WOMEN'S DIVISION I

2016 **Connecticut**	2004 **Connecticut**	1992 **Stanford**
2015 **Connecticut**	2003 **Connecticut**	1991 **Tennessee**
2014 **Connecticut**	2002 **Connecticut**	1990 **Stanford**
2013 **Connecticut**	2001 **Notre Dame**	1989 **Tennessee**
2012 **Baylor**	2000 **Connecticut**	1988 **Louisiana Tech**
2011 **Texas A&M**	1999 **Purdue**	1987 **Tennessee**
2010 **Connecticut**	1998 **Tennessee**	1986 **Texas**
2009 **Connecticut**	1997 **Tennessee**	1985 **Old Dominion**
2008 **Tennessee**	1996 **Tennessee**	1984 **USC**
2007 **Tennessee**	1995 **Connecticut**	1983 **USC**
2006 **Maryland**	1994 **North Carolina**	1982 **Louisiana Tech**
2005 **Baylor**	1993 **Texas Tech**	

NBA

THIS ONE'S FOR CLEVELAND

LeBron James hoisted the NBA championship trophy after making a dream come true. He came back to the Cleveland Cavaliers with one goal: to bring a title to his hometown area. James led his team to a record-breaking comeback win over the Golden State Warriors in the NBA Finals. (See page 99.)

2015-16 Season

Kawhi Leonard led the Spurs to a team record.

After thousands of dribbles, points, dunks, and assists, and hundreds of exciting games, the NBA season came down to a repeat. The game's two best players led the two best teams to a thrilling NBA Finals. The one thing that was new? The champion. To the surprise of everyone except fans in Cleveland, **LeBron James** and the Cavaliers beat the record-setting Golden State Warriors in seven games to win the city's first pro sports title of any kind since 1964.

Though the Warriors were disappointed in the end, they had a season for the ages. Their 73 regular-season victories set an NBA record, topping the 72 wins of the Chicago Bulls in 1995–96. **Stephen Curry** won his second consecutive league MVP award while putting the single-season three-point basket record out of reach. He rained down 402 treys, easily topping his one-year-old record of 286. He was aided by his "Splash Brother," fellow Warriors guard **Klay Thompson**, who was nearly as deadly from outside. The team included the fiery **Draymond Green**, a force on offense and defense; inside man **Andre Iguodala**, another great defender; big man **Andrew Bogut**; and a deep bench. The team's motto: "Strength in Numbers." Its strongest number: 73!

The Western Conference, in which the Warriors play, was packed with the best teams not from Cleveland. The San Antonio Spurs won a franchise record 67 games. The Spurs won their first 39 home games of the season—an NBA record. Over a portion of the 2014–15 and 2015–16 seasons, they won 49 consecutive games at home. Who snapped that streak? The Warriors, who won their 72nd game of the season while ending the Spurs' home success. Also in the West, **Kevin Durant** and the Oklahoma City Thunder came within a whisker of beating the Warriors in the playoffs. (How the Thunder will fare in 2016–17 after Durant signed with the Warriors is a story to follow.) The Los Angeles Clippers stormed through the regular season, but key injuries crushed their hopes in the playoffs.

In the East, Cleveland was clearly the top team. The Cavaliers went through the conference playoffs with a 12–2 record. However, here's a shout-out to the Toronto Raptors, who won those two playoff games against Cleveland. In the regular season, the Raptors won a team record 56 games.

Great Start!

The Golden State Warriors won the NBA championship in the 2014–15 season, and they kept rolling as the 2015–16 season began. They won 24 consecutive games to start the season, a new all-time record. Amazingly, they were led by a fill-in coach. Head coach **Steve Kerr** had back surgery and could not be with the team, so **Luke Walton** took over. (Walton's success earned him the Los Angeles Lakers' head coaching job for 2016–17!) The Warriors' great start played a big part in their record 73-win season.

Not Great Start!

While the Warriors started hot, the Philadelphia 76ers were positively arctic! They set a record no one wants, losing their first 18 games of the season. After a win over the Lakers, Philly lost another 12 in a row. By Christmas, the 76ers' record was 1–30! Their fans want to put the 10–72 season in the "do-over" column!

2015–2016 FINAL STANDINGS

EASTERN CONFERENCE

ATLANTIC DIVISION	W–L
Raptors	56–26
Celtics	48–34
Knicks	32–50
Nets	21–61
76ers	10–72

CENTRAL DIVISION	W–L
Cavaliers	57–25
Pacers	45–37
Pistons	44–38
Bulls	42–40
Bucks	33–49

SOUTHEAST DIVISION	W–L
Heat	48–34
Hawks	48–34
Hornets	48–34
Wizards	41–41
Magic	35–47

WESTERN CONFERENCE

NORTHWEST DIVISION	W–L
Thunder	55–27
Trail Blazers	44–38
Jazz	40–42
Nuggets	33–49
Timberwolves	29–53

PACIFIC DIVISION	W–L
Warriors	73–9
Clippers	53–29
Kings	33–49
Suns	23–59
Lakers	17–65

SOUTHWEST DIVISION	W–L
Spurs	67–15
Mavericks	42–40
Grizzlies	42–40
Rockets	41–41
Pelicans	30–52

2016 NBA Playoffs

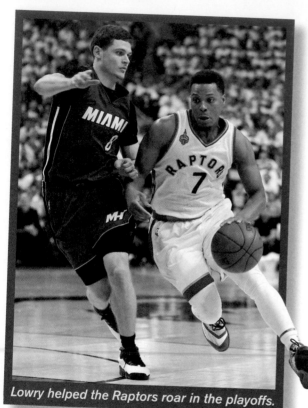

Lowry helped the Raptors roar in the playoffs.

round, the Cavs kept rolling, sweeping the Atlanta Hawks. . . . The other Eastern semifinal was a terrific series, with both the Miami Heat and the Raptors showing their best. Toronto won Game 7 behind 35 points from **Kyle Lowry** to advance. . . . The best semifinal matchup in the West was the six-game clash between the Thunder and the Spurs. In front of his home fans, Oklahoma City's **Kevin Durant** poured in 37 points in the clinching game. San Antonio and its 67 regular-season wins went home.

CONFERENCE FINALS

WEST: The Thunder almost pulled off an upset. They had the 73-win Warriors on the ropes, ahead three games to one. Only nine other teams had come back from such a playoff deficit, but the Warriors made it 10. Golden State had to win Game 6 in Oklahoma City in front of some of the NBA's loudest fans. The Warriors did it with an all-around game, and in spite of the play of the Thunder's **Kevin Durant** and **Russell Westbrook**. Golden State won Game 7 at home 96–88 to advance to its second consecutive NBA Finals.

EAST: Toronto handed Cleveland its first losses in the playoffs (Cleveland had swept its first two opponents), but the Cavaliers' power was still too much for the Raptors. **LeBron James** scored 33 points and grabbed 11 rebounds as Cleveland romped 113–87 on the road in Game 6 to seal the series. The Cavs were the highest-scoring team in the playoffs to this point, and all signs looked good for a fierce NBA Finals battle . . . again!

EARLY ROUNDS

The San Antonio Spurs and the Cleveland Cavaliers rolled to sweeps in the first round. . . . The Los Angeles Clippers lost stars **Blake Griffin** and **Chris Paul** to injury and were upset by the Portland Trail Blazers. . . . The eighth-seeded Rockets managed to win a game against the Warriors, but Golden State put Houston away in Game 5. . . . The Indiana Pacers took the Raptors to seven games, but Toronto won Game 7 for its first series win since 2001. . . . In the second

2016 NBA Finals

GAME 1
Warriors 104, Cavaliers 89
The Splash Brothers–**Stephen Curry** and **Klay Thompson**–were the Ice-Cold Brothers, but the Warriors' supporting cast picked them up. **Shaun Livingston** scored 20 points and **Draymond Green** added 16.

GAME 2
Warriors 110, Cavaliers 77
Cleveland never got started in this rout. It was only the second time that a **LeBron James** team fell behind two games to none in a playoff series. "The King" had only 19 points and also had 7 turnovers.

GAME 3
Cavaliers 120, Warriors 90
The Cavs did to the Warriors what the Warriors had done to the Cavs! James poured in 32 points and grabbed 11 boards in front of Cleveland's excited home fans. It was a remarkable turnaround after the Cavaliers' Game 2 defeat.

GAME 4
Warriors 108, Cavaliers 97
Curry was back on his game, scoring 38 points, including 7 three-pointers. Those treys were part of an NBA Finals-record 17 made by Golden State. Guard **Kyrie Irving** had 34 points for the Cavs.

GAME 5
Cavaliers 112, Warriors 97
Green was suspended because of 4 flagrant fouls during the postseason, and the Cavs feasted inside. On the Warriors' home court, James (41 points) and Irving (also 41) became the first NBA teammates to score 40 or more points each in an NBA Finals game.

GAME 6
Cavaliers 115, Warriors 101
Back in Cleveland, things went the Cavs' way again. A frustrated Curry fouled out, then was ejected after complaining about the calls. James scored 41 points again as Cleveland forced Game 7.

GAME 7
Cavaliers 93, Warriors 89
It was a classic. The teams were neck-and-neck throughout. But Curry was not sharp, and James was determined. Late in the fourth quarter, he made a key block of a shot by **Andre Iguodala**. Irving made a tie-breaking three-point basket, and Cleveland held on for an historic win. James, naturally, was named the Finals MVP.

James had Curry's number in the Finals.

NBA Awards

ALL THE VOTES!

For the first time in NBA history, a player got all the first-place votes for the Most Valuable Player award. Golden State's Stephen Curry repeated as the MVP, and voting for him was easy! He shattered his own record for three-point baskets with 402, plus led his team to an all-time record 73 wins. Curry also led the league in scoring for the first time, with a 30.1 points-per-game average, and was also tops in free throw percentage and steals per game. Wow!

❝The guy is unbelievable. It's like playing in real life against a guy from a video game.❞ –GORAN DRAGIC, MIAMI HEAT

NBA AWARDS

ROOKIE OF THE YEAR	**Karl-Anthony TOWNS**, Timberwolves
DEFENSIVE PLAYER OF THE YEAR	**Kawhi LEONARD**, Spurs
SIXTH MAN	**Jamal CRAWFORD**, Clippers
MOST IMPROVED	**C. J. McCOLLUM**, Trail Blazers
ALL-STAR GAME MVP	**Russell WESTBROOK**, Thunder
COACH OF THE YEAR	**Steve KERR**, Warriors

NBA Stat Leaders

Most NBA stats are ranked "per game" (pg). That is, the numbers below represent the average each player had for all his games in 2015–16.

30.1 POINTS (PPG)
2.14 STEALS (SPG)
90.8 FREE THROW PCT.
Stephen Curry, Warriors

11.7 ASSISTS (APG)
Rajon Rondo, Kings

14.8 REBOUNDS (RPG)
Andre Drummond, Pistons

70.3 FIELD GOAL PCT.
DeAndre Jordan, Clippers

3.7 BLOCKS (BPG)
Hassan Whiteside, Heat

4.9 OFF. REBOUNDS (ORPG)
Andre Drummond, Pistons

402

That's the new single-season record for three-point baskets set by the amazing **Stephen Curry**. It is a shockingly high number. One stat expert compared that to a baseball player slugging 103 homers in a season!

In the Paint

Golden State was not the only team making news in the NBA. Here are some memorable non-Warriors (mostly!) headlines from the 2015–16 season.

50! James "The Beard" Harden took advantage of the Philadelphia 76ers' slow start to score his season-high 50 points for the Houston Rockets in a November win.

Check It Twice! The
Portland Trail Blazers had to play a January game against the Clippers without C. J. McCollum, their second-leading scorer. He wasn't hurt, but he had to sit because of a mistake in some paperwork! Teams have to give officials a roster of active players

60 minutes before the game. By mistake, McCollum was not listed as active on that sheet, so he was not allowed to play. Portland missed him, losing 109–98.

Tough Town Cleveland fired head
coach David Blatt in January, even though his team was in first place in its division with a 30–11 record! Tyronn Lue took over and led the team to the NBA championship.

All-Star Fun Once again,
defense took the night off at the annual NBA All-Star Game. The Western Conference beat the Eastern Conference 196–173! Oklahoma City's Russell Westbrook had 31 points for the West and was the MVP for the second year in a row. Indiana's Paul George scored 41 points, 1 short of an All-Star Game record, for the East. The Lakers' Kobe Bryant, who retired at the end of the season, set a record with his 15th consecutive start.

◀◀◀Up and Down Chicago
Bulls star Jimmy Butler scored a career-high 53 points on January 14 against the 76ers. All that scoring must have tired him out, because he scored a season-low 4 points the next night against Dallas. That was tied for the fewest points ever in a game following a 50-point outburst!

Free! Free! Free! Toronto's
DeMar DeRozan took full advantage of the free throws the Portland Trail Blazers

Good-bye, Kobe

What a way to go out! **Kobe Bryant** hung up his sneakers after the 2015–16 season. He won five NBA titles with the Lakers and ranks third on the NBA's all-time scoring list. He played in 18 All-Star Games, starting a record 15 in a row. "The Black Mamba" was one of the best players ever, but he might have saved his best for last. Though playing on sore legs at the end of a long final season, Bryant thrilled his fans by scoring 60 points in an upset win over the Utah Jazz. Next stop: the Naismith Memorial Basketball Hall of Fame.

gave him in a game on March 4. The Raptors' guard made 24 in a row, setting an NBA record. (He missed the last of his 25 free throws in the game.) Toronto won 117–115.

Big Guy, Big Night ▶▶▶

On February 21, **Anthony Davis** of the New Orleans Pelicans scored 59 points and grabbed 20 rebounds in a victory over the Detroit Pistons. He became only the third NBA player in the last 50 years to score 55 or more points and grab 20 or more rebounds in the same game.

Non-Kobe Game of the Year?

The Warriors and Thunder put on an epic show in a February game. It was an exciting, high-scoring event. OKC's **Kevin Durant** tied a career high with 7 three-pointers, and Golden State's **Stephen Curry** had to come back from rolling his ankle in the second half. As time wound down, the Thunder led 103–99 with 15 seconds left. But the Warriors tied the game and forced overtime. In OT, Curry had the last word, draining a shot from 32 feet to win the game 121–118 and set a new single-season record for three-point baskets.

2015 WNBA

Delle Donne (left) was the league's best.

As the WNBA started its 19th season, some teams faced big challenges, while others rose to new heights.

In the West, defending champ Phoenix started the season with bad news: no **Diana Taurasi**. When not with Phoenix, Taurasi plays for a team in Russia. That team pays her 15 times more than she makes in the WNBA, and it asked the former league MVP to take the WNBA season off to rest—and even paid her entire WNBA salary! Phoenix still had the mighty **Brittney Griner**, however, and made it to the Western Conference playoffs. Seattle lost star **Lauren Jackson** to knee surgery and had one of its worst seasons ever.

In the East, the New York Liberty were the big story. One of the league's original teams, they put together their best season ever in 2015. They had the best record (23–11) in the league for the first time. Top scorer **Tina Charles** was the big star for the Liberty, who roared into the playoffs aiming for the top. But a surprise upset by the Indiana Fever in the Eastern Conference finals sent them home disappointed. New York even led in a key Game 2 by 18 points, only to see the Fever rally back. In the deciding game of that series, **Marissa Coleman** made 5 three-point baskets to lead the Fever to the Finals.

Chicago, led by WNBA MVP **Elena Delle Donne**, was another hot team. Delle Donne's all-around game includes sharp outside shooting with great post-up moves, using her height and long reach. However, the Sky fell to Indiana in the playoffs, too. Not even Della Donne's 40 points in the deciding game were enough.

2015 AWARDS AND LEADERS

MVP: **Elena Delle Donne**, Chicago
ROOKIE OF THE YEAR: **Jewell Loyd**, Seattle
DEFENSIVE PLAYER OF THE YEAR: **Brittney Griner**, Phoenix
SCORING: **Elena Delle Donne**, Chicago, 23.4 ppg
ASSISTS: **Courtney Vandersloot**, Chicago, 5.8 apg
REBOUNDS: **Courtney Paris**, Tulsa, 9.3 rpg

2015 WNBA FINALS

For the third time in five seasons, the Minnesota Lynx came out on top in the WNBA Finals. But the Indiana Fever made them work for every W.

GAME 1 Fever 75, Lynx 69
The Fever stunned the Western Conference champs, with **Briann January** scoring 19 points to lead the way.

GAME 2 Lynx 77, Fever 71
Minnesota roared back to win Game 2. Superstar **Maya Moore** scored more than half of the Lynx's fourth-quarter points, helping them hold on in a tough, physical game.

GAME 3 Lynx 80, Fever 77
Minnesota coach **Cheryl Reeve** said that this win by her team might be "one of the best WNBA Finals games" ever. A back-and-forth contest, it was not decided until Moore buried a three-pointer with 1.7 seconds left.

Fowles was the WNBA Finals MVP.

GAME 4 Fever 75, Lynx 69
Veteran forward **Tamika Catchings** only had 10 points, but it was her determined leadership that kept the Fever from going home. They forced a deciding Game 5.

GAME 5
Lynx 69, Fever 52
The first Game 5 in the WNBA Finals since 2009 started out slow. Both teams' defenses dominated, resulting in a 27–21 halftime score in favor of the Lynx. It was the lowest halftime score in WNBA Finals history. In the second half, though, the Lynx soared. **Sylvia Fowles** stepped up with 20 points to lead the way.

2015 WNBA FINAL STANDINGS

EASTERN CONFERENCE		WESTERN CONFERENCE	
New York	23-11	Minnesota	22-12
Chicago	21-13	Phoenix	20-14
Indiana	20-14	Tulsa	18-16
Washington	18-16	Los Angeles	14-20
Atlanta	15-19	Seattle	10-24
Connecticut	15-19	San Antonio	8-26

Stat Stuff

NBA CHAMPIONS

2015-16 Cleveland	2000-01 LA Lakers	1985-86 Boston
2014-15 Golden State	1999-00 LA Lakers	1984-85 LA Lakers
2013-14 San Antonio	1998-99 San Antonio	1983-84 Boston
2012-13 Miami	1997-98 Chicago	1982-83 Philadelphia
2011-12 Miami	1996-97 Chicago	1981-82 LA Lakers
2010-11 Dallas	1995-96 Chicago	1980-81 Boston
2009-10 LA Lakers	1994-95 Houston	1979-80 LA Lakers
2008-09 LA Lakers	1993-94 Houston	1978-79 Seattle
2007-08 Boston	1992-93 Chicago	1977-78 Washington
2006-07 San Antonio	1991-92 Chicago	1976-77 Portland
2005-06 Miami	1990-91 Chicago	1975-76 Boston
2004-05 San Antonio	1989-90 Detroit	1974-75 Golden State
2003-04 Detroit	1988-89 Detroit	1973-74 Boston
2002-03 San Antonio	1987-88 LA Lakers	1972-73 New York
2001-02 LA Lakers	1986-87 LA Lakers	1971-72 LA Lakers

1970-71 **Milwaukee**	1953-54 **Minneapolis**	1949-50 **Minneapolis**
1969-70 **New York**	1952-53 **Minneapolis**	1948-49 **Minneapolis**
1968-69 **Boston**	1951-52 **Minneapolis**	1947-48 **Baltimore**
1967-68 **Boston**	1950-51 **Rochester**	1946-47 **Philadelphia**
1966-67 **Philadelphia**		
1965-66 **Boston**		
1964-65 **Boston**		
1963-64 **Boston**		
1962-63 **Boston**		
1961-62 **Boston**		
1960-61 **Boston**		
1959-60 **Boston**		
1958-59 **Boston**		
1957-58 **St. Louis**		
1956-57 **Boston**		
1955-56 **Philadelphia**		
1954-55 **Syracuse**		

WNBA CHAMPIONS

2015 **Minnesota**	2005 **Sacramento**
2014 **Phoenix**	2004 **Seattle**
2013 **Minnesota**	2003 **Detroit**
2012 **Indiana**	2002 **Los Angeles**
2011 **Minnesota**	2001 **Los Angeles**
2010 **Seattle**	2000 **Houston**
2009 **Phoenix**	1999 **Houston**
2008 **Detroit**	1998 **Houston**
2007 **Phoenix**	1997 **Houston**
2006 **Detroit**	

NHL

PHOTO OP

After a hard-fought playoff series, the Pittsburgh Penguins finally got time to relax. They brought a friend: their brand-new Stanley Cup! Pittsburgh won its fourth NHL championship, knocking off the San Jose Sharks.

NHL Shoots…and Scores!

The 2015–16 NHL season was full of action, excitement, and plenty of surprises. It had new faces on coaching staffs and on the ice, and even a new arena for one of the teams to call home.

Before the season began, the NHL made two major rule changes. A lot of fans weren't happy with how important the shootout had become. (A shootout occurs when a tie game during the regular season is still deadlocked after a five-minute overtime period.) Some people said teams tried to keep the overtime scoreless in order to win in the shootout. To reduce the number of shootouts, the NHL changed to a three-on-three OT period. It used to be four-on-four. The change gave players more open ice in which to skate, and it made for more creative plays. The plan worked: The number of games that went to shootouts went down!

The other big rule change let coaches ask refs to review goals on video if they believed the play was offside, or if a player interfered with the goalie. The first goal challenged was scored by the Montreal Canadiens against the Toronto Maple Leafs on opening night. Maple Leafs coach **Mike Babcock** challenged . . . and won! The goal didn't count.

Babcock made headlines in the summer, even before the season started, by announcing that he was joining the Maple Leafs after 10 seasons as the Detroit Red Wings' head coach. The Red Wings are one of the most successful teams in recent NHL history, and the Maple Leafs are one of the least successful. Babcock, who is considered by many experts to be the league's best coach, became the highest-paid coach in the NHL. Detroit, under new coach **Jeff Blashill**, made

The NHL faced off in Brooklyn, New York, for the first time.

Three-on-three was just fine with these Blues.

way to another great season after starting off with a red-hot 9–0 record. Unfortunately, Price was injured in November and was out for the season. Without him, the Canadiens went 29–38–6 the rest of the way, missing the playoffs for the first time since 2012. In fact, the 2015–16 NHL season was the first time since 1970 that no teams from Canada made the playoffs.

The New York Islanders made a big change, moving from the Nassau Coliseum, their home since 1972, to the Barclays Center in Brooklyn, New York. Not everyone was happy with the move. Many fans complained. They said it was hard to get there and some seats did not have good views. Players grumbled about the ice quality. It didn't bother the Islanders much, though, as they finished with 100 points and made the playoffs.

The NHL playoffs were a whole new hockey game, as usual. Seven of the eight teams that finished in first or second place in their divisions went home early. In the end, a flightless bird stood alone with the Stanley Cup!

the playoffs for the 25th consecutive season. Toronto did not reach the postseason.

In 2014–15, the Montreal Canadiens were one of the best teams in the league, led by MVP goalie **Carey Price**. The Canadiens looked like they were on their

FINAL STANDINGS

EASTERN CONFERENCE

ATLANTIC DIVISION	PTS	METROPOLITAN DIV.	PTS
Florida	103	Washington	120
Tampa Bay	97	Pittsburgh	104
Detroit	93	NY Rangers	101
Boston	93	NY Islanders	100
Ottawa	85	Philadelphia	96
Montreal	82	Carolina	86
Buffalo	81	New Jersey	84
Toronto	69	Columbus	76

WESTERN CONFERENCE

CENTRAL DIVISION	PTS	PACIFIC DIVISION	PTS
Dallas	109	Anaheim	103
St. Louis	107	Los Angeles	102
Chicago	103	San Jose	98
Nashville	96	Arizona	78
Minnesota	87	Calgary	77
Colorado	82	Vancouver	75
Winnipeg	78	Edmonton	70

Stanley Cup Playoffs

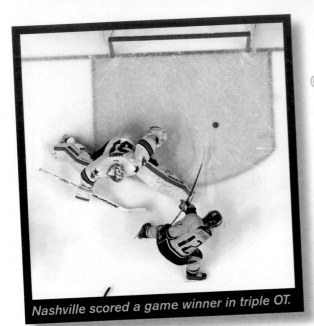

Nashville scored a game winner in triple OT.

Hedman were terrific, and the Islanders were sent home after five games.

◎ When the NHL's highest-scoring team, the Dallas Stars, played the Blues, one of the best defensive teams, the stage was set for a great series. Two games were decided in overtime. In a tense Game 7, the Blues scored 3 goals in the first period and went on to win 6–1 and knock out the Stars.

◎ The San Jose Sharks jumped out to an early lead over the Nashville Predators in the series. The Predators battled back to tie it, including an electrifying triple overtime win. In Game 7, Sharks goalie **Martin Jones** made 20 saves on his way to a shutout victory.

FIRST-ROUND HIGHLIGHTS

◎ The New York Islanders won their first playoff series in 23 years. They beat the Florida Panthers in six games—the last two wins came in double overtime.

◎ The St. Louis Blues knocked out the Chicago Blackhawks, the defending Stanley Cup champions, in an exciting seven-game series.

SECOND ROUND

◎ The Tampa Bay Lightning were missing two of their best players—**Steven Stamkos** and **Anton Stralman**—when they faced off against the Islanders. But Lightning goalie **Ben Bishop** and star defenseman **Victor**

CONFERENCE CHAMPIONSHIPS

EASTERN: The Lightning, which won the Eastern Conference in 2014–15, faced the Penguins. It was a battle of young goalies. The lead in the series went back and forth before rookie surprise **Bryan Rust** scored 2 goals in Game 7 to send Pittsburgh to the Stanley Cup Finals.

WESTERN: This match-up pitted the stingy defense of the Blues against the powerhouse offense of the Sharks. The Sharks got big scores from team captain **Joe Pavelski** and veteran **Joe Thornton**, and sensational goaltending from **Martin Jones**. They knocked out the Blues in six games. The Sharks headed to the first Stanley Cup Final appearance in their 25-year history.

Penguin Power!
STANLEY CUP FINALS

The Pittsburgh Penguins and the San Jose Sharks displayed speed, skill, and muscle in the finals. The Penguins smothered Sharks scorers by blocking dozens of shots, while Sharks goaltender Martin Jones faced a barrage but kept the series close with acrobatic saves. Each team gave its fans plenty of excitement.

GAME 1: Penguins 3, Sharks 2

The Penguins jumped out to a 2–0 lead in the first period, but the Sharks battled back with 2 goals in the second. The game remained tied until Pittsburgh's **Nick Bonino** snapped a shot past **Martin Jones** with less than three minutes to play.

GAME 2: Penguins 2, Sharks 1 (OT)

Great scoring chances, outstanding saves, and several shots ringing off posts left the game tied 1–1 after three periods. Early in the overtime, Penguins center **Sidney Crosby** won a face-off and slid the puck to **Kris Letang**. He passed it to rookie playoff sensation **Conor Sheary**, who fired a shot over Jones's shoulder to give the Penguins the win and a 2–0 series lead.

GAME 3: Sharks 3, Penguins 2 (OT)

The Sharks erased the Penguins' 2–1 lead with a third-period blast from **Joel Ward** that sent the game into overtime. Sharks fans got loud when rookie forward **Joonas Donskoi** fired home a shot in the extra period to win the game.

GAME 4: Penguins 3, Sharks 1

The Penguins got off to another fast start with a first-period goal by **Ian Cole**. They continued to block Sharks shots, and added

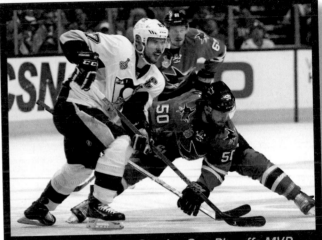

Crosby (left) was the Stanley Cup Playoffs MVP.

a goal by **Evgeni Malkin** in the second period. The Penguins won and moved within one game of claiming the Stanley Cup.

GAME 5: Sharks 4, Penguins 2

The Sharks refused to go home. Led by Jones's great goaltending (he faced 46 shots), they won 4–2. It was a wild contest with a combined 5 goals scored in the first period—4 of them in just over the first five minutes.

GAME 6: Penguins 3, Sharks 1

Crosby made a perfect pass from behind the net to Letang, who banged home a second-period goal that was the game winner as the Penguins clinched the Cup.

Hockey Highlights

Record Netter

The Washington Capitals had a season to remember in 2015–16, racking up 56 wins and 120 points. That was tops in the NHL in the regular season. The Capitals' man in goal, **Braden Holtby**, was a big reason for their success. Holtby had an outstanding season, tying **Martin Brodeur**'s single-season record for wins (48) by a goaltender.

Super Streak!

Patrick Kane recorded a point in 26 consecutive games, the longest streak since 1992 and a record for American-born players. The streak was snapped in a 3–0 loss to the Colorado Avalanche. Late in the season, Kane scored a hat trick (3 goals in a single game) against the Boston Bruins to hit the 100-point mark for the first time in his nine-year career.

WOMEN'S HOCKEY SCORES!

NWHL action between the Riveters and the Whale.

* The National Women's Hockey League debuted in October 2015. The first season featured the Boston Pride, the New York Riveters, the Connecticut Whale, and the Buffalo Beauts going after the Isobel Cup, named for Lord Stanley's daughter. The Pride defeated the Beauts in the finals to win the first NWHL title!

* The gold-medal match of the 2016 International Ice Hockey Federation Women's World Championship pitted the United States against Canada. It was a rematch of the 2014 Olympic gold-medal game, which Canada won. This time, the United States came out on top, 7–5. **Brianna Decker** scored the go-ahead goal. **Hilary Knight** dominated the tournament with 12 points in just five games!

Good-bye, Mr. Hockey

When **Gordie Howe** passed away at age 88 in June 2016, Hall of Fame coach **Scotty Bowman** said, "If you were ever going to make a mold for a hockey player with five strengths—offense, defense, durability, toughness, and versatility—you wouldn't look past Gordie Howe. He was the best ever." Many agreed. Nicknamed "Mr. Hockey," Howe scored 801 career goals and played until he was 52 years old.

Old Guys Rock!

Jaromir Jagr turned 44 on February 15, 2016, but he's showing no signs of slowing down. The Czech superstar became the oldest player ever to score 60 points in a season, leading Florida with 66. That helped the Panthers win a division title and reach the playoffs for the first time since 2012. Jagr also scored his 742nd goal and his 1,851st point during the season, moving to third in NHL history in both categories.

All-Star Surprises

The 2016 NHL All-Star Game was held in Nashville, with a major change in format. It became a four-team tournament, with one team from each division. The three tournament "games" were 20-minute, three-on-three contests. Also, fans got to vote for the four team captains. Picking up on a joke made on a sports podcast, fans flooded the balloting with votes for the Arizona Coyotes' **John Scott** in the Pacific Division. The forward had 5 goals, 6 assists, and 542 penalty minutes in his eight-year NHL career. The NHL was grumpy about the voting. But even after he was traded to Montreal and sent to the minor leagues, the NHL let him play as captain of the Pacific Division team in the four-team event. He scored twice and was named MVP! The fans loved it!

Chewy? The Sharks' Brent Burns.

2015-16 Awards

Hart Trophy
(Most Valuable Player)
Lindsay Award
(MVP as voted by the players)
Art Ross Trophy
(Top Point Scorer)
PATRICK KANE, Blackhawks ▶

Maurice Richard Trophy
(Top Goal Scorer)
ALEX OVECHKIN, Capitals

Norris Trophy
(Best Defenseman)
DREW DOUGHTY, Kings

Vezina Trophy
(Best Goaltender)
BRADEN HOLTBY, Capitals

Calder Trophy
(Rookie of the Year)
ARTEMI PANARIN, Blackhawks

Jack Adams Award
(Best Coach)
BARRY TROTZ, Capitals

Selke Trophy
(Best Defensive Forward)
Lady Byng Trophy
(Sportsmanship and Ability)
ANZE KOPITAR, Kings

" It's amazing to be the first American, because there have been so many great players from the US."
— PATRICK KANE

Kane was the first American ever to win the MVP award.

Masterton Trophy
(Perseverance and Dedication to Hockey)
JAROMIR JAGR, Panthers

Messier Leadership Award
(Leadership On and Off the Ice)
SHEA WEBER, Predators

Stat Leaders

106 POINTS
Patrick Kane, Blackhawks

50 GOALS
19 POWER-PLAY GOALS
Alex Ovechkin, Capitals

66 ASSISTS
28:58 AVG. ICE TIME
Erik Karlsson, Senators

35 PLUS/MINUS
Tyler Toffoli, Kings

177 PENALTY MINUTES
Derek Dorsett, Canucks
Alex Ovechkin, Capitals

2.06 GOALS AGAINST AVG.
.926 SAVE PERCENTAGE
Ben Bishop, Lightning ▶▶▶

48 GOALIE WINS
Braden Holtby, Capitals

49.7

That's the percentage of NHL players in 2015–16 who were from Canada . . . the lowest ever! Americans were 24.2 percent, while Swedes set a new high at 9.1 percent.

Stanley Cup Champions

2015–16	**Pittsburgh Penguins**		1989–90	**Edmonton Oilers**
2014–15	**Chicago Blackhawks**		1988–89	**Calgary Flames**
2013–14	**Los Angeles Kings**		1987–88	**Edmonton Oilers**
2012–13	**Chicago Blackhawks**		1986–87	**Edmonton Oilers**
2011–12	**Los Angeles Kings**		1985–86	**Montreal Canadiens**
2010–11	**Boston Bruins**		1984–85	**Edmonton Oilers**
2009–10	**Chicago Blackhawks**		1983–84	**Edmonton Oilers**
2008–09	**Pittsburgh Penguins**		1982–83	**New York Islanders**
2007–08	**Detroit Red Wings**		1981–82	**New York Islanders**
2006–07	**Anaheim Ducks**		1980–81	**New York Islanders**
2005–06	**Carolina Hurricanes**		1979–80	**New York Islanders**
2004–05	No champion (Lockout)		1978–79	**Montreal Canadiens**
2003–04	**Tampa Bay Lightning**		1977–78	**Montreal Canadiens**
2002–03	**New Jersey Devils**		1976–77	**Montreal Canadiens**
2001–02	**Detroit Red Wings**		1975–76	**Montreal Canadiens**
2000–01	**Colorado Avalanche**		1974–75	**Philadelphia Flyers**
1999–00	**New Jersey Devils**		1973–74	**Philadelphia Flyers**
1998–99	**Dallas Stars**		1972–73	**Montreal Canadiens**
1997–98	**Detroit Red Wings**		1971–72	**Boston Bruins**
1996–97	**Detroit Red Wings**		1970–71	**Montreal Canadiens**
1995–96	**Colorado Avalanche**		1969–70	**Boston Bruins**
1994–95	**New Jersey Devils**		1968–69	**Montreal Canadiens**
1993–94	**New York Rangers**		1967–68	**Montreal Canadiens**
1992–93	**Montreal Canadiens**		1966–67	**Toronto Maple Leafs**
1991–92	**Pittsburgh Penguins**		1965–66	**Montreal Canadiens**
1990–91	**Pittsburgh Penguins**		1964–65	**Montreal Canadiens**

MOST STANLEY CUP TITLES

Montreal Canadiens	**24**
Toronto Maple Leafs	**13**
Detroit Red Wings	**11**
Boston Bruins	**6**
Chicago Blackhawks	**6**

Season	Champion
1963–64	**Toronto Maple Leafs**
1962–63	**Toronto Maple Leafs**
1961–62	**Toronto Maple Leafs**
1960–61	**Chicago Blackhawks**
1959–60	**Montreal Canadiens**
1958–59	**Montreal Canadiens**
1957–58	**Montreal Canadiens**
1956–57	**Montreal Canadiens**
1955–56	**Montreal Canadiens**
1954–55	**Detroit Red Wings**
1953–54	**Detroit Red Wings**
1952–53	**Montreal Canadiens**
1951–52	**Detroit Red Wings**
1950–51	**Toronto Maple Leafs**
1949–50	**Detroit Red Wings**
1948–49	**Toronto Maple Leafs**
1947–48	**Toronto Maple Leafs**
1946–47	**Toronto Maple Leafs**
1945–46	**Montreal Canadiens**
1944–45	**Toronto Maple Leafs**
1943–44	**Montreal Canadiens**
1942–43	**Detroit Red Wings**
1941–42	**Toronto Maple Leafs**
1940–41	**Boston Bruins**
1939–40	**New York Rangers**
1938–39	**Boston Bruins**
1937–38	**Chicago Blackhawks**
1936–37	**Detroit Red Wings**
1935–36	**Detroit Red Wings**

Season	Champion
1934–35	**Montreal Maroons**
1933–34	**Chicago Blackhawks**
1932–33	**New York Rangers**
1931–32	**Toronto Maple Leafs**
1930–31	**Montreal Canadiens**
1929–30	**Montreal Canadiens**
1928–29	**Boston Bruins**
1927–28	**New York Rangers**
1926–27	**Ottawa Senators**
1925–26	**Montreal Maroons**
1924–25	**Montreal Canadiens**
1923–24	**Montreal Canadiens**
1922–23	**Ottawa Senators**
1921–22	**Toronto St. Patricks**
1920–21	**Ottawa Senators**
1919–20	**Ottawa Senators**
1918–19	**Montreal Canadiens**
1917–18	**Toronto Arenas**

SOCCER

HATS OFF TO RONALDO!

Soccer saw a lot of big moments and important tournaments in 2016, but perhaps the biggest moment came at the European Championships. Superstar Cristiano Ronaldo helped Portugal win its first title . . . and the trophy he wore!

2015 MLS Recap

MLS Notes

→ **Happy Anniversary!:** MLS celebrated its 20th season in 2015. That's not bad for a league many "experts" didn't expect to last long. MLS had its best year in 2015, averaging more than 21,000 fans per game. That's more than leagues in Argentina and France! The 20-team MLS continues to grow and has plans to jump to 24 teams by 2020. Eventually, the league expects to grow to 28 teams.

→ **Good Start, Old Man:** Former Premier League star **Didier Drogba** joined MLS in 2015, playing for the Montreal Impact. He made an immediate impact! Drogba scored a hat trick—that's 3 goals in a game—in his first start. At 37, he was also the oldest MLS player ever to produce a hat trick.

→ **English Flavor:** Two of the biggest names in English soccer moved to MLS in 2015. Longtime Liverpool hero **Steven Gerrard** played for the Galaxy. **Frank Lampard**, Chelsea's all-time leading scorer, played for the New York City Football Club.

→ **MVP, Italian Style:** The MLS MVP was another big-name player from Europe. **Sebastian Giovinco** of Toronto FC scored 22 goals and had an MLS-best 16 assists. He was named the winner of the **Landon Donovan** MVP trophy and won the Golden Boot as top scorer. Giovinco tied Columbus' **Kei Kamara** for the league lead in goals scored, but had more assists.

→ **Good-bye Galaxy:** The defending-champion Galaxy looked like they would have a great shot at repeating. If only they didn't have to play the final month of the season! Los Angeles went winless in eight

Drogba (right) showed he still had his world-class moves.

Portland's Jack Jewsbury hoisted the MLS Cup.

" I don't think it has sunk in yet that there's no next game . . . We're the best team in MLS this year!"

– CALEB PORTER, PORTLAND TIMBERS COACH

a pair of goals in the second match to knock off Vancouver after the teams played to a scoreless tie in the first leg.

Conference Finals: In the West, Portland won the first leg 3–1 over FC Dallas, then qualified to play for the MLS Cup with a 2–2 tie in the second leg. The Timbers and their devoted fans reached the MLS Cup for the first time. In the East, Columbus held on to beat the New York Red Bulls. The Crew won the first leg 2–0, and advanced despite a 1–0 loss in the second leg. The second leg was very tense, and Columbus needed a last-minute defensive stand to hold on.

of its final nine matches, which knocked the club out of first place. The Galaxy had to play a knockout-round match to advance, but lost 3–2 on the road to rival Seattle. It was a disappointing end for a star-studded team.

MLS Playoffs

Semifinals: The two-leg semifinal round, which decided the teams that advanced to the conference finals, contained lots of late drama. FC Dallas shocked the Seattle Sounders by winning in penalty kicks in front of the home crowd. Columbus needed a goal in the 111th minute to defeat Montreal. The New York Red Bulls got an injury-time goal in their victory over DC United. In a game with less late action, Portland scored

MLS Cup

With a better regular-season record than Portland, Columbus played host to the MLS Cup. The home field did not prove to be an advantage. A terrible mistake by Crew goalie **Steve Clark** led to a Timbers goal by **Diego Valeri** just 27 seconds into the match! It was the earliest goal scored in the 20-year history of the big game. Portland scored again about six minutes later on a sharp header by defender **Rodney Wallace**. The early goals shocked the Crew and their fans. Columbus got one back from star **Kei Kamara**, but that was all it could manage. In its first-ever MLS Cup, Portland carried home the trophy with a 2–1 win.

2016 Champions League

Gareth Bale and Cristiano Ronaldo led Real to victory.

Barcelona and Bayern Munich on the way to the final.

In the championship match, **Sergio Ramos** put Real ahead with a goal in the first half. Atlético's **Yannick Carrasco** then tied the score. No one else could break through, and the game remained tied through 30 minutes of extra time.

In the penalty-kick shootout, an Atlético player clanged his shot off the goalpost. That left it to—who else?—Ronaldo to step up and power home the championship-winning goal for Real's 11th title.

The top club teams in Europe played the Champions League to see who was the best. As the final match began, the answer was clear: The winner would be Madrid. That's because both teams that made the championship match—Real Madrid and Atlético Madrid—play in the Spanish capital.

Real Madrid was led by the amazing **Cristiano Ronaldo**, who scored 16 goals in the Champions League. During the team's Spanish League season, he became the club's all-time leading scorer. Real had also won the most championships in this competition, 10, dating to the first event in 1955.

Atlético was a bit of a surprise. It knocked off top teams such as

Quarterfinals

▸ **Manchester City** over **Paris St.-Germain**

▸ **Real Madrid** over **Wolfsburg**

▸ **Bayern Munich** over **Benfica**

▸ **Atlético Madrid** over **Barcelona**

Semifinals

▸ **Real Madrid** over **Manchester City**

▸ **Atlético Madrid** over **Bayern Munich**

Final

▸ **Real Madrid 1, Atlético Madrid 1**
Real won 5–3 on penalty kicks

Copa América Centenario

Francisco Silva of Chile celebrated.

The World Cup is the most famous soccer tournament in the world. But it's not the oldest! That honor goes to the Copa América, played mostly among South and Central American nations. In 2016, it celebrated its 100th anniversary, called *Centenario* in Spanish. For the first time, it was played in the United States, a nation that has occasionally taken part in the event. Sixteen teams made it to the finals. The biggest upset was that Brazil did not make it out of group play. A 1–0 loss to Peru knocked out Brazil. Another surprise was that the US team won its group, clinching it with a big win over Paraguay. Then the Americans made the semifinals with a huge win over Ecuador. **Clint Dempsey** scored 5 goals for the US team in the tournament. In the quarterfinals, Chile shocked Mexico with a 7–0 win, embarrassing a team that thought it had a chance to win it all.

Semifinals: The US was no match for **Lionel Messi** and Argentina. The world's best player curled in an unstoppable free kick to lead his team to a 4–0 win. In the other semifinal, Chile made it past Colombia 2–0. That set up a rematch of the 2015 Copa final.

Championship: A shocking ending! Argentina and Chile tied 0–0. In the penalty-kick shootout, the sun didn't rise, the Earth stopped spinning, and dogs loved cats. In other words, Messi missed a penalty kick! His shot soared over the goal! Chile won the shootout and its second straight Copa América. After the game, Messi said he was retiring from the national team . . . but we'll see if he changes his mind!

. . . Messi didn't.

Euro's Underdogs

In world soccer, the giants usually come out on top. Nations with histories of winning most often do just that when it comes time to win the big events. Underdogs rarely take home trophies. But at the 2016 UEFA European Championships, underdogs were the biggest story of all.

Twenty-four teams from Europe played at stadiums across France. Fans were treated to some amazing goals and action from some of the game's biggest stars. But it was the underdogs that got the headlines. First, tiny Iceland tied Portugal, which was led the by the great **Cristiano Ronaldo**. When Iceland then tied Hungary, the bandwagon filled up quickly. Fans around the world marveled at a country with just about 330,000 people doing well against nations 10 times as large. Wales was another small country doing well, surprising Slovakia and Russia. That put Wales into the second round of a major tournament for the first time since 1958! Then Iceland shocked again, beating Austria to reach the round of 16 for the first time. The Viking chant of the devoted Iceland fans swept the world!

In the round of 16, order was mostly restored. Germany, Italy, France, Poland, and Belgium advanced to the quarterfinals. But look who else slipped in: Portugal, which had never won the European Championships before; Wales, which beat Northern Ireland; and Iceland, which shocked England! Then Wales blew past Belgium. Could the Red Dragons make the final? No, Ronaldo was too much. He led Portugal to the championship match. Home nation France ended Iceland's dream, then beat Germany to reach the final, too. Early in the final, Portugal found itself in trouble when Ronaldo had to leave with a knee injury. But neither side could score in regulation play. In extra time, **Éder** of Portugal smashed home a long shot for the game's only goal. Ronaldo and Portugal finally had their trophy . . . one for the underdogs!

Gareth Bale, Wales star

Premier League
Soccer Shocker!

Jamie Vardy held the trophy few thought his team could win.

Soccer has been played in England for more than 150 years. It has seen lots of amazing feats, but none quite as amazing as what Leicester City did in 2016. First, for us American fans, it is pronounced "LESS-ter." Second, in English soccer, teams that finish at the bottom are demoted to a lower league each year. Top teams from lower leagues move up. When the 2015–16 season began, Leicester City was only one year away from nearly moving down a league. The club was a 5,000–1 underdog to win the championship. No one, not even its biggest fans, could have imagined what happened next.

The Foxes, as the Leicester City team is called, started winning. They were near the top of the standings in January. Then they were in first place. "It can't last," nearly everyone said. But the Foxes, who were led by top scorer **Jamie Vardy**, kept right on winning. At one point, Vardy set an all-time Premier League record by scoring a goal in 11 consecutive matches! As the matches went on, it became an international story. Soccer fans around the world jumped on the Leicester bandwagon. When its two closest pursuers tied a game in May, Leicester City had clinched the first title of any kind in its 132-year history. It was a Foxes shocker!

Women's Pro Soccer

Helped by players from the US team that won the Women's World Cup, the National Women's Soccer League had a solid season in 2015. Nine teams played a 20-game schedule. In the championship game, US World Cup player **Amy Rodriguez** (right) scored the only goal as FC Kansas City defeated the Seattle Reign. **Nicole Barnhart**, a goalie on the American World Cup squad, made key saves for Kansas City.

Stat Stuff

MAJOR LEAGUE SOCCER
CHAMPIONS

2015 Portland Timbers
2014 Los Angeles Galaxy
2013 Sporting Kansas City
2012 Los Angeles Galaxy
2011 Los Angeles Galaxy
2010 Colorado Rapids
2009 Real Salt Lake
2008 Columbus Crew
2007 Houston Dynamo
2006 Houston Dynamo
2005 Los Angeles Galaxy
2004 DC United
2003 San Jose Earthquakes
2002 Los Angeles Galaxy
2001 San Jose Earthquakes
2000 Kansas City Wizards
1999 DC United
1998 Chicago Fire
1997 DC United
1996 DC United

UEFA CHAMPIONS
LEAGUE

The Champions League pits the best against the best. The top club teams from the members of UEFA (Union of European Football Associations) face off in a months-long tournament.

2016 Real Madrid SPAIN
2015 FC Barcelona SPAIN
2014 Real Madrid SPAIN
2013 Bayern Munich GERMANY
2012 Chelsea FC ENGLAND
2011 FC Barcelona SPAIN
2010 Inter (Milan) ITALY
2009 FC Barcelona SPAIN
2008 Manchester United ENGLAND
2007 AC Milan ITALY
2006 FC Barcelona SPAIN
2005 Liverpool FC ENGLAND
2004 FC Porto PORTUGAL
2003 AC Milan ITALY
2002 Real Madrid SPAIN
2001 Bayern Munich GERMANY

WOMEN'S WORLD CUP

YEAR	CHAMPION	RUNNER-UP
2015	**United States**	Japan
2011	**Japan**	United States
2007	**Germany**	Brazil
2003	**Germany**	Sweden
1999	**United States**	China
1995	**Norway**	Germany
1991	**United States**	Norway

COPA AMÉRICA ALL-TIME WINNERS

Chile won the 100th edition of the Copa América. Here are the teams that have won the most titles in the event's history.

TITLES	NATION	MOST RECENT
15	**Uruguay**	2011
14	**Argentina**	1993
8	**Brazil**	2007
2	**Chile**	2016
2	**Paraguay**	1979
2	**Peru**	1975

Chile won its titles in 2015 and 2016.

NASCAR

SUPER CLOSE FINISH!
Denny Hamlin (11) nipped Martin Truex Jr. (78) by less than a foot to win the 2016 Daytona 500 in the closest finish in the race's long history.

Kyle Comeback!

Kyle Busch (arrow) returned from this bad crash to create an amazing comeback story.

NASCAR drivers face huge pressure every race day. They battle each other in metal monsters moving at insane speeds, inches away from concrete walls and each other. It's an emotional and intense sport. The occasional scuffle in the pits after a race is not that unusual.

So imagine having to do all that while dealing with a broken leg!

The day before the 2015 Daytona 500, Kyle Busch was racing in the lower-division Xfinity series. A crash left him with a broken right leg and left foot. A season in which he was expected to contend for a title suddenly looked doubtful.

Busch missed the first 11 races of the Sprint Cup season as he recovered.

NASCAR made a special ruling that if he won a race, he would still qualify for the Chase, even though he would not have run enough races. Busch took care of the win by capturing the road race at Sonoma in June.

In July, he proved he was back for good by winning three races in a row. He won the Quaker State 400 at Kentucky and then in the 5-hour Energy 301 at New Hampshire. He capped the streak with a huge victory in the Jeff Kyle 400 at the famous Indianapolis Motor Speedway. That put him solidly in place for the Chase.

Once the Chase began (see page 134), Busch was sure and steady. He put together a series of strong finishes, though he didn't win any more races . . . until the last one. In Miami, as one of the "final four," Busch roared to a double "W"—winning the race and, with it, his first NASCAR championship. It completed a remarkable comeback for a gutsy driver.

The season-ending race also marked the last for one of NASCAR's all-time greats. Jeff Gordon finished third in the Chase to wrap up a season-long, race-by-race farewell tour. The four-time champion (1995, 1997, 1998, and 2001), one of NASCAR's most famous drivers, said good-bye to his fans at track after track. From 1994 to 2015, he finished in the top 10 in points every season except one (and in that one, in 2005, he was 11th!). Nicknamed the "Rainbow Warrior" after an early sponsor's logo, Gordon will be remembered as one of the best ever.

With more courageous championship performances like he had in 2015, will Kyle Busch have a chance to "be like Jeff"?

CHASE FOR THE CUP
2015 FINAL STANDINGS

1. **Kyle BUSCH**
2. **Kevin HARVICK**
3. **Jeff GORDON**
4. **Martin TRUEX JR.**
5. **Carl EDWARDS**
6. **Joey LOGANO**
7. **Brad KESELOWSKI**
8. **Kurt BUSCH**
9. **Denny HAMLIN**
10. **Jimmie JOHNSON**
11. **Ryan NEWMAN**
12. **Dale EARNHARDT JR.**
13. **Jamie McMURRAY**
14. **Paul MENARD**
15. **Matt KENSETH**

Gordon waved good-bye after an outstanding career.

93

Jeff Gordon (right) retired in 2015 with 93 race wins, good for third all-time behind **Richard Petty** (200) and **David Pearson** (105).

The Chase

The Chase for the Cup pits the top 16 racers in NASCAR's playoffs. A win in one of the races guarantees advancement. High finishes help, too. But in each round, some drivers are dropped, leaving the "final four" to race for the season title in Miami. The winner of each race is listed after the track site.

Challenger Round

CHICAGO: Denny Hamlin. Kyle Busch led for 121 laps, but Hamlin punched his ticket to the next round.

NEW HAMPSHIRE: Matt Kenseth. Kenseth won for the fifth time in 2015 and stayed in first place overall.

DOVER: Kevin Harvick. The defending champ kept alive his hopes for a repeat title. He was out front for 355 of the 400 laps at Dover.

OUT: Jimmie Johnson, Paul Menard, Jamie McMurray, Clint Bowyer

Contender Round

CHARLOTTE: Joey Logano. The young driver wasted no time earning a berth in the next round, winning at Charlotte for his fourth victory of the season.

KANSAS: Logano. After this race, Logano wasn't going to be getting a holiday card from Kenseth. Already set for the next round, Logano made a late pass that spun Kenseth out of the lead. A win would have sent Kenseth through to the Eliminator Round; instead, he remained in last place and needed to win at Talladega.

Kevin Harvick was shooting for two season titles in a row after his win at Dover.

TALLADEGA: Logano. NASCAR fans were shocked when their hero, Dale Earnhardt Jr., was knocked out of first place in the race—and knocked out of the Chase—by a controversial yellow-flag caution on the last lap.

OUT: Dale Earnhardt Jr., Matt Kenseth, Ryan Newman, Denny Hamlin

Eliminator Round

MARTINSVILLE: Jeff Gordon. In his final NASCAR season, Gordon earned a shot at his fifth title. He won for the ninth time at Martinsville to clinch a spot in the season-ending championship race in Miami.

TEXAS: Jimmie Johnson. The six-time champ was out of contention for the 2015 championship, but he showed he could still win races by roaring to his fifth victory of the season.

PHOENIX: Dale Earnhardt Jr. The final four for the Chase for the Sprint Cup was determined by this race! Although rain shortened the race, the standings were set. The four drivers who qualified to race for the Cup in Miami: four-time champ Jeff Gordon, 2014 winner Kevin Harvick, four-race winner Kyle Busch, and underdog Martin Truex Jr.

OUT: Carl Edwards, Joey Logano, Kurt Busch, Brad Keselowski

Kyle Busch captures a NASCAR trophy selfie!

Sprint Cup Championship

MIAMI: Kyle Busch. Jeff Gordon's fairy-tale ending didn't happen. Martin Truex Jr.'s out-of-nowhere Cinderella story ended. Kevin Harvick couldn't make it two in a row. That left the championship epic to be written by a driver who battled back from serious injuries to win the biggest race of all. After missing nearly three months of racing, Busch won four times to earn his spot in the final four. At Miami, he held off Harvick's late charge to win the race and his first NASCAR Sprint Cup title.

Kyle and Kurt Busch (2004) joined Terry (1984, 1996) and Bobby Labonte (2000) as the only brothers to win the NASCAR season title.

Other NASCAR Champs

2015 Xfinity Series

Kyle Busch led the way with six race wins, but he spends most of his time in the Sprint Cup series, so he wasn't eligible to capture this title, too! Fellow Sprint Cup driver **Austin Dillon** won four Xfinity races. Among eligible drivers, **Chris Buescher** (above) put up a pair of wins as part of 20 top-10 finishes. He ended with 1,190 points to win his first series championship. **Chase Elliott**, who moved up to the Sprint Cup in 2016, finished second.

CAMPING WORLD TRUCK SERIES

Does he ever take a day off? **Kyle Busch** won a pair of races in this truck series, too! **Erik Jones** drove home with the championship, however. He was lights-out in the second half of the season, finishing in the top 10 in each of the final 15 races, including three victories. **Tyler Reddick** won two of the first six races but couldn't hold off the fast-charging Jones.

Around the Track

Squeaking In

The last race before the 2015 Chase began determined the final spots in the season-ending playoffs. Matt Kenseth won the event in Richmond. He joined Kyle Busch and Jimmie Johnson for the season lead to that point with four wins. Near the back of the pack, however, was the real story. Paul Menard ended up in 26th place, but that gave him enough points to earn his first try at the Chase.

Happy's Happy Year

Kevin "Happy" Harvick was the 2014 champ, and he almost made it two in a row. He had the best season of any driver other than Kyle Busch. Harvick won a trio of races and was in the top five 23 times! Look for him to keep challenging for the season title for many years.

Classic Colors ▶▶▶

At the 2015 Southern 500, NASCAR jumped into a time machine. The cars all used "throwback" designs based on legendary drivers of the past. Ricky Stenhouse Jr.'s No. 17 looked like David Pearson's famous car. Alex Bowman put on stickers to make his car look like an old-time "modified" vehicle. And was that Richard Petty back on the track in car No. 43? No, it was just Aric Almirola in a car painted to look like the one driven by "The King."

Toyota on Top

Kyle Busch's championship was the first for carmaker Toyota. Based in Japan, the company joined NASCAR in 2007. It has long been involved in auto racing around the world and was part of IndyCar in the United States. But when it entered NASCAR, many longtime fans were not sure. NASCAR is the classic "American" racing series, but Toyota has proved it belongs. Its cars have won many other types of races, and the company now joins American carmakers such as Chevrolet, Ford, Chrysler, and others as NASCAR champions.

2016 Notes

TWO CLOSE!

In the last 10 seasons before 2016, NASCAR had seen only one race end with the winner ahead by just 1/100th of a second. But then it had two such races in less than two months. First, the 2016 Daytona 500 went down to the wire. **Denny Hamlin** nipped **Martin Truex Jr.** by less than a foot for his first win in the fabled race. Then, a month later, **Kevin Harvick** held off hard-charging **Carl Edwards** to win in Phoenix. The two bumped and banged down the final stretch before Harvick nosed ahead.

STEWART Says So Long

NASCAR said good-bye to another legendary driver in 2016. **Tony Stewart** announced plans to retire at the end of the season. Stewart won three NASCAR season championships (2002, 2005, and 2011) and took the checkered flag in 48 races in his 17 seasons entering 2016. He battled injuries in recent years and missed the first part of the 2016 season with a back injury suffered while riding an ATV in the sand. He'll be remembered for his ability to drive just about anything. He won titles in go-karts, sports cars, trucks, and midget cars, along with his Sprint Cup success.

LOOOONG DAY!

The Coca-Cola 600 is NASCAR's longest race. In the 2016 running at Charlotte, **Martin Truex Jr.** didn't mind the extra laps. He broke a four-year victory drought with a dominating performance. In fact, he led 588 of the 600 laps, the most laps ever led by a driver in a NASCAR race!

Digital Dashboard Debuts

NASCAR drivers need a lot of information to win. In 2016, they got a new way to take it all in when NASCAR rolled out digital dashboard displays in all its cars. Before this new high-tech gear came into use, cars could only use mechanical dials that were not much different from those used dozens of years ago. The new displays give drivers information on speed, lap and race time, fuel, oil pressure, and more. Drivers can customize the display to work with their driving styles, too. Crew chiefs and drivers were excited to see how this new tech would help them win more races!

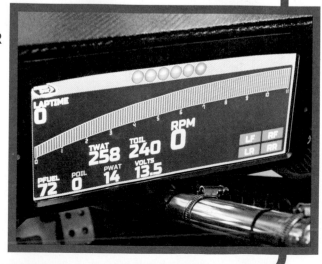

NASCAR Champions

YEAR	DRIVER	CAR MAKER	YEAR	DRIVER	CAR MAKER
2015	Kyle Busch	Toyota	1994	Dale Earnhardt Sr.	Chevrolet
2014	Kevin Harvick	Chevrolet	1993	Dale Earnhardt Sr.	Chevrolet
2013	Jimmie Johnson	Chevrolet	1992	Alan Kulwicki	Ford
2012	Brad Keselowski	Dodge	1991	Dale Earnhardt Sr.	Chevrolet
2011	Tony Stewart	Chevrolet	1990	Dale Earnhardt Sr.	Chevrolet
2010	Jimmie Johnson	Chevrolet	1989	Rusty Wallace	Pontiac
2009	Jimmie Johnson	Chevrolet	1988	Bill Elliott	Ford
2008	Jimmie Johnson	Chevrolet	1987	Dale Earnhardt Sr.	Chevrolet
2007	Jimmie Johnson	Chevrolet	1986	Dale Earnhardt Sr.	Chevrolet
2006	Jimmie Johnson	Chevrolet	1985	Darrell Waltrip	Chevrolet
2005	Tony Stewart	Chevrolet	1984	Terry Labonte	Chevrolet
2004	Kurt Busch	Ford	1983	Bobby Allison	Buick
2003	Matt Kenseth	Ford	1982	Darrell Waltrip	Buick
2002	Tony Stewart	Pontiac	1981	Darrell Waltrip	Buick
2001	Jeff Gordon	Chevrolet	1980	Dale Earnhardt Sr.	Chevrolet
2000	Bobby Labonte	Pontiac	1979	Richard Petty	Chevrolet
1999	Dale Jarrett	Ford	1978	Cale Yarborough	Oldsmobile
1998	Jeff Gordon	Chevrolet	1977	Cale Yarborough	Chevrolet
1997	Jeff Gordon	Chevrolet	1976	Cale Yarborough	Chevrolet
1996	Terry Labonte	Chevrolet	1975	Richard Petty	Dodge
1995	Jeff Gordon	Chevrolet	1974	Richard Petty	Dodge

YEAR	DRIVER	CAR MAKER	YEAR	DRIVER	CAR MAKER
1973	Benny Parsons	Chevrolet	1960	Rex White	Chevrolet
1972	Richard Petty	Plymouth	1959	Lee Petty	Plymouth
1971	Richard Petty	Plymouth	1958	Lee Petty	Oldsmobile
1970	Bobby Isaac	Dodge	1957	Buck Baker	Chevrolet
1969	David Pearson	Ford	1956	Buck Baker	Chrysler
1968	David Pearson	Ford	1955	Tim Flock	Chrysler
1967	Richard Petty	Plymouth	1954	Lee Petty	Chrysler
1966	David Pearson	Dodge	1953	Herb Thomas	Hudson
1965	Ned Jarrett	Ford	1952	Tim Flock	Hudson
1964	Richard Petty	Plymouth	1951	Herb Thomas	Hudson
1963	Joe Weatherly	Pontiac	1950	Bill Rexford	Oldsmobile
1962	Joe Weatherly	Pontiac	1949	Red Byron	Oldsmobile
1961	Ned Jarrett	Chevrolet			

2017 NASCAR HALL OF FAME CLASS

Richard Childress: A partnership with fellow Hall of Famer Dale Earnhardt Sr. helped this car owner rack up 11 NASCAR championships, second-most all-time.

Rick Hendrick: This car owner racked up 14 top-series championships, the most ever, thanks in large part to great drivers such as Jimmie Johnson (6 titles) and Jeff Gordon (4).

Mark Martin: Forty NASCAR race wins and 49 Xfinity Series wins (second-best all-time) is a great résumé for this Hall of Fame driver. Active past the age of 50, he finished second in the overall season standings five times.

Raymond Parks: The early days of NASCAR were the stomping grounds of this car owner. He and driver Red Byron teamed to win the first NASCAR title in 1949. Parks's cars won dozens of races in the 1940s and 1950s.

Benny Parsons: The 1975 Daytona 500 title was a career highlight for this longtime driver. He finished in the top 10 in more than half his races.

OTHER MOTOR SPORTS

INDY TURNS 100

A lot of things have changed since the first Indy 500 in 1911. Ray Harroun won the first one in a Marmon Wasp (above). In May 2016, Alexander Rossi won the 100th Indy 500 (page 147) in a machine built by Honda. The cars are very different, but the goal is still the same: speed through 500 miles on a huge track faster than all the other drivers!

Formula 1

The amazing Lewis Hamilton of Great Britain won his third Formula 1 drivers' championship.

The exciting, globe-hopping Formula 1 racing season was a three-driver battle in 2015 among **Lewis Hamilton**, **Nico Rosberg**, and **Sebastian Vettel**. Great Britain's Hamilton was the defending champion everyone was chasing. Germany's Rosberg had been the runner-up in the points race in 2014 and had seven top-10 finishes in his career, but he was seeking his first title. And fellow German Vettel was already a four-time champion. As it turned out, those three drivers won all 19 races in the 2015 season.

Hamilton got off to a hot start while chasing his third career title. He won three of the first four races of the year. Vettel captured the other, in Malaysia. Rosberg nosed into contention with his own stretch of three victories in four races: Spain, Monaco, and Austria. In the Monaco race, Hamilton looked like a sure winner until a late-race pit stop went wrong and cost him valuable time, letting Rosberg fly ahead.

Hamilton then matched Rosberg's streak by winning at Silverstone in his home

> **❝I owe it all to my dad and family who supported me all these years and sacrificed so much for me to be here, and my fans who give me so much positive energy. ❞**
>
> — LEWIS HAMILTON

country, in Belgium, and in Italy. Vettel squeezed in with wins in Hungary and Singapore.

In October, Hamilton won at Sochi, Russia, setting up a chance to clinch the season championship two weeks later in Austin, Texas, at the US Grand Prix. It was only the second season back on the circuit for a US track, and Hamilton and Rosberg gave the fans a great show. **Daniel Ricciardo** and **Daniil Kvyat** joined the chase in Austin, making for rare, tight-packed action in a sport that doesn't see a lot of lead changes. Rosberg was ahead late, until he slid off the track at a tight corner. Hamilton zoomed ahead and won the race. The checkered flag gave him enough points to ensure the season championship.

Rosberg won the final three races of the 2015 season—and never let up on the gas. He opened 2016 by winning the first four races!

Hamilton ended 2015 with 10 race wins, followed by Rosberg with 6 and Vettel with 3. Rosberg finished at No. 2 in the standings for the second straight season.

Rosberg was hot late in '15 and early in '16.

Vettel's third-place finish overall was a return to form after he won four consecutive titles from 2010 to 2013. Among the teams, Mercedes was the clear leader, with 16 wins from its titanic twosome of Hamilton and Rosberg.

2015 F1 FINAL STANDINGS

DRIVER	COUNTRY	TEAM	POINTS
1. Lewis HAMILTON	Great Britain	Mercedes	381
2. Nico ROSBERG	Germany	Mercedes	322
3. Sebastian VETTEL	Germany	Ferrari	278
4. Kimi RÄIKKÖNEN	Finland	Ferrari	150
5. Valtteri BOTTAS	Finland	Williams	136
6. Felipe MASSA	Brazil	Williams	121
7. Daniil KVYAT	Russia	Red Bull Racing	95
8. Daniel RICCIARDO	Australia	Red Bull Racing	92
9. Sergio PEREZ	Mexico	Force India	78
10. Nico HÜLKENBERG	Germany	Force India	58

2015 IndyCar

Sometimes slow and steady can win in auto racing. Well, maybe not slow—but steady, for sure! That was the case in 2015, when **Scott Dixon** captured his fourth IndyCar title. Dixon won only three races and was in the top three in just one other race, but he put together enough high finishes to end up tied with **Juan Pablo Montoya** for the most points. Dixon earned the season title on a tiebreaker: His three wins were more than Montoya's two.

The season started with a bit of a bump. The race in Brazil was canceled by Brazilian government authorities in a political argument. In April, the circuit raced in New Orleans for the first time. **James Hinchcliffe** was the winner. He was one of five different drivers who won the season's first five races. In all, nine drivers won at least one of the 16 races in 2015. Two drivers won their first career races: American **Josef Newgarden** at Birmingham and Colombia's **Carlos Muñoz** at Detroit. Late in May, Montoya won the 99th running of the Indy 500 in a three-car battle on the last lap.

The IndyCar world was shocked late in the season by the death of **Justin Wilson** from injuries suffered in a race at Pocono. He was hit by debris from another car. But it's a dangerous sport; the racing went on.

In a stunning finish to the season, Scott Dixon roared from behind to snatch the IndyCar title.

2016 INDY 500
100 EQUALS 1

The Indy 500 is one of the most famous auto races in the world. In 2016, more than 300,000 people packed the Indianapolis Motor Speedway to watch the 100th running of the race. **Ray Harroun** won the first Indy 500 way back in 1911. His average speed was 74.6 mph, which was pretty fast back then! In 2016, American **Alexander Rossi** made his first IndyCar win a memorable one. He averaged 161 mph, but wasn't going that fast at the end. Rossi ran out of fuel just after he passed the finish line, which is made of bricks in honor of the track's heritage as the "Brickyard." Rossi also continued a long Indy tradition by drinking from a bottle of milk after reaching Victory Lane. The California native was the first IndyCar rookie to win the race since 2001.

Heading into the final race at Sonoma in California, Montoya led in total points. In fact, he had led nearly all year, but he needed to finish strong to capture the title. If Dixon, in third place in the standings, could win, he might catch Montoya.

The star from New Zealand put himself in position to win, grabbing the lead a little more than halfway through the race and holding it lap after lap. Montoya hit another car and lost a lot of time. Still, if he could squeeze into fifth place, he would have enough points to win. He battled, but could not move up enough. His sixth-place finish, combined with Dixon's win, left the two drivers tied with 556 points. **Will Power**, the defending champ, came in third overall. **Graham Rahal**, who had started the day in second overall, had a bad race and finished fourth on the season.

Dixon's four IndyCar titles tied him with **Dario Franchitti** for the most ever.

2015 VERIZON INDYCAR SERIES
FINAL STANDINGS

DRIVER	POINTS
1. **Scott DIXON**	*556
2. Juan Pablo **MONTOYA**	556
3. **Will POWER**	493
4. Graham **RAHAL**	490
5. Helio **CASTRONEVES**	453

*Dixon won championship on a tiebreaker.

Drag Racing

Pink power! Antron Brown roared to the title in Top Fuel.

TOP FUEL

Like NASCAR, the NHRA has a countdown to its championship. The top drivers face off over the final six weeks, with one emerging in each division as the champ. In Top Fuel—the most famous series in the sport thanks to the long, thin, odd-looking cars—the 2015 title could have gone to several drivers. But once the countdown races started, one star quickly emerged. **Antron Brown** won the first three races in the championship and capped it off with his second Top Fuel title. The former motorcycle racer also won in 2012.

FUNNY CAR

Like Top Fuel's Antron Brown, Funny Car's **Del Worsham** picked the right time to get hot. Unlike Brown, who had won four events heading into the countdown, Worsham did not win any . . . until the first two in the countdown! He won two of the next four as well, powering to his first Funny Car title. Worsham is also a former Top Fuel champ, making him only the third driver to win titles in two different divisions.

PRO STOCK

At the end of the 2015 Pro Stock countdown, the trophy had the same name on it as the year before. **Erica Enders-Stevens** won three of the six countdown races to grab her second Pro Stock title in a row. A year earlier, she became the first woman to win the division—now she is the first to win twice! Her victory was not a big surprise; she won a division-leading six events during the season leading up to the finals.

PRO STOCK MOTORCYCLE

For **Andrew Hines**, drag racing is all in the family. His dad, **Byron**, is a Hall of Fame driver, and his brother, **Matt**, is a three-time champ in the motorcycle division. But in 2015, Andrew added another page to the family story. By winning his fifth championship, he tied the great **Dave Schultz** for most ever by a two-wheel drag racer. His 42 race wins are second on the all-time list behind Schultz, too. Looks like dad won't be the only Hines in the Hall of Fame!

Motorcycle Racing

MOTOCROSS

Finish strong! That's the path to success in the mud-churning, outdoor racing action of the Lucas Oil Pro Motocross series. At the series finale in 2016, the Ironman in Illinois, **Ken Roczen** did that and more. Roczen had battled injuries and accidents since winning the 2014 title and wanted to return to the top spot. He had a sizable points lead heading into the Ironman, but had to . . . finish strong. He sure did, winning both motos while avoiding the crashes and mechanical problems of other riders. Roczen grew up in Germany racing minibikes and came to America with the goal of becoming a champion. With his second title, he certainly has a place among the world's top riders!

MUD MANIA!

Most champions don't want to end their seasons covered in mud and with a damaged motorcycle. But that's how **Ryan Dungey** capped off his second consecutive AMA Supercross title. He had already clinched the title a week before the final race in Las Vegas. But in that event, a massive rainstorm turned the outdoor track into a mud pit! Dungey crashed early in the final race with **Ken Roczen**. But he got back on the battered bike, wiped off his goggles, and sprinted ahead to complete another winning season!

Motocross of Nations

For almost 70 years, the best motocross riders in the world have gathered to represent their countries at the Motocross of Nations. Teams of three riders take part in a series of three races that ends with one nation atop the standings. The 2015 event was held in France, and the host nation thrilled its fans by beating 35 other national teams to win its second consecutive title. French riders **Gautier Paulin**, **Marvin Musquin**, and **Romain Febvre** (right) squeaked into first, just two points ahead of Team USA (**Jeremy Martin**, **Justin Barcia**, and **Cooper Webb**).

Major Champions
OF THE 2000s

TOP FUEL DRAGSTERS

YEAR	DRIVER
2015	Antron Brown
2014	Tony Schumacher
2013	Shawn Langdon
2012	Antron Brown
2011	Del Worsham
2010	Larry Dixon
2009	Tony Schumacher
2008	Tony Schumacher
2007	Tony Schumacher
2006	Tony Schumacher
2005	Tony Schumacher
2004	Tony Schumacher
2003	Larry Dixon
2002	Larry Dixon
2001	Kenny Bernstein

FUNNY CARS

YEAR	DRIVER
2015	Del Worsham
2014	Matt Hagan
2013	John Force
2012	Jack Beckman
2011	Matt Hagan
2010	John Force
2009	Robert Hight
2008	Cruz Pedregon
2007	Tony Pedregon
2006	John Force
2005	Gary Scelzi
2004	John Force
2003	Tony Pedregon
2002	John Force
2001	John Force

PRO STOCK CARS

YEAR	DRIVER
2015	Erica Enders-Stevens
2014	Erica Enders-Stevens
2013	Jeg Coughlin Jr.
2012	Allen Johnson
2011	Jason Line
2010	Greg Anderson
2009	Mike Edwards
2008	Jeg Coughlin Jr.
2007	Jeg Coughlin Jr.
2006	Jason Line
2005	Greg Anderson
2004	Greg Anderson
2003	Greg Anderson
2002	Jeg Coughlin Jr.
2001	Warren Johnson

FORMULA 1

YEAR	DRIVER
2015	Lewis Hamilton
2014	Lewis Hamilton
2013	Sebastian Vettel
2012	Sebastian Vettel
2011	Sebastian Vettel
2010	Sebastian Vettel
2009	Jenson Button
2008	Lewis Hamilton
2007	Kimi Räikkönen
2006	Fernando Alonso
2005	Fernando Alonso
2004	Michael Schumacher
2003	Michael Schumacher
2002	Michael Schumacher
2001	Michael Schumacher

INDYCAR SERIES

YEAR	DRIVER
2015	Scott Dixon
2014	Will Power
2013	Scott Dixon
2012	Ryan Hunter-Reay
2011	Dario Franchitti
2010	Dario Franchitti
2009	Dario Franchitti
2008	Scott Dixon
2007	Dario Franchitti
2006	Sam Hornish Jr.
2005	Dan Wheldon
2004	Tony Kanaan
2003	Scott Dixon
2002	Sam Hornish Jr.
2001	Sam Hornish Jr.

AMA SUPERCROSS

YEAR	DRIVER
2016	Ryan Dungey
2015	Ryan Dungey
2014	Ryan Villopoto
2013	Ryan Villopoto
2012	Ryan Villopoto
2011	Ryan Villopoto
2010	Ryan Dungey
2009	James Stewart Jr.
2008	Chad Reed
2007	James Stewart Jr.
2006	Ricky Carmichael
2005	Ricky Carmichael
2004	Chad Reed
2003	Ricky Carmichael
2002	Ricky Carmichael
2001	Ricky Carmichael

AMA MOTOCROSS

YEAR	RIDER (MOTOCROSS)	RIDER (LITES)
2016	Ken Roczen	Cooper Webb
2015	Ryan Dungey	Jeremy Martin
2014	Ken Roczen	Jeremy Martin
2013	Ryan Villopoto	Eli Tomac
2012	Ryan Dungey	Blake Baggett
2011	Ryan Villopoto	Dean Wilson
2010	Ryan Dungey	Trey Canard
2009	Chad Reed	Ryan Dungey
2008	James Stewart Jr.	Ryan Villopoto
2007	Grant Langston	Ryan Villopoto
2006	Ricky Carmichael	Ryan Villopoto
2005	Ricky Carmichael	Ivan Tedesco
2004	Ricky Carmichael	James Stewart Jr.
2003	Ricky Carmichael	Grant Langston
2002	Ricky Carmichael	James Stewart Jr.
2001	Ricky Carmichael	Mike Brown

ACTION SPORTS

DON'T WORRY!
Rob Adelberg performed this trick during warmups for the 2016 Summer X Games Moto X Freestyle event. Rob has some mad skills, but he finished second in the event. For more results, turn the page!

Summer X Games

The weather was the X factor at the Summer X Games in Austin, Texas. Early June thunderstorms, plus some lightning, wrecked the schedule. But with help from lots of volunteers using towels and squeegees, the patient—but wet—crowds saw some amazing action sports . . . action!

From the Hospital to Gold

Australia's **Jacko Strong** proved to be as good as his name. During Moto X QuarterPipe, he crashed his bike. He hurt his neck and doctors were so worried, they sent him right to the hospital. Jacko was sore but not seriously hurt. So he hopped into a helicopter, flew back to the X Games, and won a gold medal in Moto X Best Trick! Proving Americans can be tough, too, **Axell Hodges** popped his shoulder out in Moto X Step Up, but returned to earn a silver medal in Best Whip.

◀◀◀ Quite a Feat

Action sports are mostly a young person's game. The sports are hard on the body and call for amazing flexibility. That makes **Bob Burnquist's** success so remarkable. In Austin, he was in his 26th X Games—he's been at every one! Though he had racked up 30 medals coming in, he didn't add to his collection this year. See you in 2017, Bob!

Clutch Performance

Garrett Reynolds is a BMX veteran. He's been around the X Games for years and has a stack of medals. But after his second run in

> **"**On my board, I feel free. This is something I can't live without.**"**
>
> – X GAMES MEDALIST
> **BRIGHTON ZEUNER**

SUMMER X GAMES GOLD MEDALISTS

BMX DIRT	**Kevin Peraza**	MOTO X QUARTERPIPE	**Tom Pagès**
BMX PARK	**Dennis Enarson**	MOTO X STEP UP	**Jarryd McNeil**
BMX STREET	**Garrett Reynolds**	M SKATEBOARD PARK	**Pedro Barros**
BMX VERT	**Jamie Bestwick**	W SKATEBOARD PARK	**Kisa Nakamura**
HARLEY-DAVIDSON FLAT TRACK	**Jared Mees**	M SKATEBOARD STREET	**Ryan Decenzo**
MOTO X BEST TRICK	**Jacko Strong**	W SKATEBOARD STREET	**Pâmela Rosa**
MOTO X BEST WHIP	**Jarryd McNeil**	SKATEBOARD ST. AMATEURS	**Tyson Bowerbank**
MOTO X FREESTYLE	**Josh Sheehan**	SKATEBOARD VERT	**Sam Beckett**

BMX Street, it looked like he had no chance for a medal in Austin. He drew on all his skills, though, and put together a fantastic third run that ended with him earning a gold medal.

Rockin' Rosa!

Brazilian teenager **Pâmela Rosa** showed the old folks who was boss in Skateboard Street. Her amazing performance gave her a gold medal to go with the one she had earned earlier in the year at the X Games in Oslo, Norway. In Austin, she outdid 2015 Female Skater of the Year **Leticia Bufoni**, another Brazilian.

Wait until She Grows Up!

At 11 years, 10 months old, women's Skateboard Park rider **Brighton Zeuner** is the youngest person ever at the X Games. She finished fourth, just one point out of a medal. She's been skating since she was five!

Rosa tasted like a winner at the X Games in Oslo, too.

Worth the Wait!

Most Summer X Games events are human-powered only. But the Harley-Davidson Flat Track event features some of the top motorcycle riders in the world ripping around a dirt track. In the 2015 event, racer **Jared Mees** led most of the race, but lost on the last lap when his chain broke. In 2016, his bike cooperated and powered him to a gold medal.

Winter X Games

One thing you need for a Winter X Games is snow. At the 2016 Aspen X Games, Mother Nature came through in a big way. In fact, there was almost too much snow after a weekend storm blanketed the mountains. The Men's Snowboard SuperPipe was so snowed under that the athletes got only one run each. Otherwise, the awesome athletes skied, 'boarded, rode, and slid through event after event. Here are some of the best stories.

New Teen Star

Kelly Sildaru was only 13 years old and was a long way from her home in Estonia. But in the women's Ski Slopestyle, she found the Colorado air to her liking. She became the youngest Winter X Games gold medalist ever with a breathtaking final run. **Chloe Kim**, the woman whose age record Kelly beat, did pretty well herself. Kim won her second consecutive Snowboard SuperPipe . . . while only 15!

◄◄◄ Wrong Way = Right Way

In Snowmobile Freestyle, **Joe Parsons** pulled off a truly amazing trick he called the Parsby Flip to clinch the gold. After zooming his machine up the ramp, he did a backflip in midair and landed on the seat of the snowmobile . . . facing backward! Somehow, he landed the machine and applied the brakes by reaching behind him! Wow!

Good Stuff

The X Games includes three events for athletes who battle not only snow, but also serious physical challenges. Athletes who are missing limbs are able to take part in Adaptive events in Snocross and

Snowboarder, as well as the Mono Skier X event. They use special gear that helps them fly down the mountains. **Mike Schultz** won his seventh gold medal in Snocross Adaptive in Aspen. Another cool event at these Games was the Special Olympics Unified snowboard slalom, where Special Olympians teamed with star snowboarders.

One Point Apart

The high-flying Ski Big Air final ended as one of the closest in the Games. Skiers do tricks while flying high in the air off a ramp. Judges give them points for skill and success. After pulling off tricks that included a triple cork 1440 safety and a triple cork 1620 safety, France's **Fabian Bösch** finished with 86 points. **Bobby Brown** of the United States had 85 points.

X Games Notes

✱ **Gus Kenworthy**, who won an Olympic silver medal in 2014, won silver medals

> *"Ever since I was a little girl, this was all I wanted. I'm so honored to be part of women's snowboarding."*
>
> –**SPENCER O'BRIEN**, WHO WON HER FIRST SNOWBOARD SLOPESTYLE GOLD AFTER 10 YEARS OF TRYING

in Aspen in both Slopestyle and SuperPipe for skiers. He was the only person to try both events in Aspen . . . and won his first-ever X Games silver medals!

✱ **Jossi Wells** from New Zealand had come oh-so-close many times in his nine previous X Games. In Aspen, he stuck his landing and won his first gold in Ski Slopestyle.

✱ **Lindsey Jacobellis** won her 10th Snowboarder X gold medal, but she had to wait out a photo finish. She edged out **Eva Samková**.

2016 WINTER X GAMES CHAMPS

MONO SKIER X	**Jerome Elbrycht**	SNOWBOARDER ADAPTIVE	**Matti Suur-Hamari**
SKI BIG AIR	**Fabian Bösch**	M SNOWBOARDER X	**Jarryd Hughes**
M SKIER X	**Brady Leman**	W SNOWBOARDER X	**Lindsey Jacobellis**
W SKIER X	**Kelsey Serwa**	M SNOWBOARD SLOPESTYLE	**Mark McMorris**
M SKI SLOPESTYLE	**Jossi Wells**	W SNOWBOARD SLOPESTYLE	**Spencer O'Brien**
W SKI SLOPESTYLE	**Kelly Sildaru**	M SNOWBOARD SUPERPIPE	**Matt Ladley**
M SKI SUPERPIPE	**Kevin Rolland**	W SNOWBOARD SUPERPIPE	**Chloe Kim**
W SKI SUPERPIPE	**Maddie Bowman**	SNOWMOBILE FREESTYLE	**Joe Parsons**
SNOCROSS ADAPTIVE	**Mike Schultz**	SNOWMOBILE SNOCROSS	**Tucker Hibbert**
SNOWBOARD BIG AIR	**Max Parrot**		

Action Notes

Surf Champs

With a victory in the final event of the season, **Adriano de Souza** of Brazil won his first World Surf League title. He overcame defending champ **Mick Fanning** of Australia to win the Pipeline Masters off the coast of Oahu, Hawaii. De Souza finished in the top five in 7 of the 11 events. Hawaii's **Carissa Moore** clinched the women's title by winning the final event. It was her fourth event victory of the season and her third world championship.

The Eddie

When the massive waves rise up from Waimea Bay, a special event is held for only the bravest and boldest big-wave surfers. It's called The Eddie, named for **Eddie Aikau**, a legendary surfer and lifeguard who lost his life in the surf. In 2016, another crop of the best board-riders in the world paddled into the surf. Even Eddie's 66-year-old brother Clyde caught some waves! After hours of incredible action, 23-year-old **John John Florence** became the youngest winner in the history of the event.

Moves like this one earned Adriano de Souza his first World Surf League championship.

Dave Mirra was a pioneer in BMX and became a worldwide star. His death was a shock.

Sad Day for BMX

Dave Mirra was the first real international superstar of BMX trick riding and racing. He earned at least one medal in every X Games from 1995 through 2009 and at one time held the record for most career medals. He invented tricks and brought the sport he loved to a wide audience. Sadly, he took his own life in early 2016. Some experts think the many crashes he went through might have affected his brain, causing changes that led to his death. Action sports fans will miss him, but hope to learn lessons about safety for the future.

Real Snow 2016

Two snowboarders took home big prizes in the Real Snow contest. They posted videos of their amazing and creative snowboarding runs—over buildings and obstacles, down ramps and slides, and through the streets. Fans and judges voted online after watching all the contestants. Judges gave the nod to **Dylan Thompson**, while the fans liked **Frank Bourgeois** best. See who you like best by searching for Real Snow 2016 videos (but just watch . . . don't copy them!).

Slide, Tom . . . Slide!

In April 2016, **Tom Wallisch** went for a new world record on a special rail-slide course made on his hometown ski run in Pennsylvania. The veteran free skier tried again and again over several days before he finally did it. After crashing over and over, he put together a 424-foot rail slide on skis—the longest ever!

GOLF

EYES ON THE PRIZE
*Henrik Stenson became the first player
from Sweden to win a men's major when
he captured the British Open after an epic
duel with Phil Mickelson.*

Major Firsts

How impressive was the duel between **Henrik Stenson** and **Phil Mickelson** at the 2016 British Open? The guy who finished in third place behind them trailed by . . . 11 strokes! The 145th Open came down to an epic battle between two great golfers. Though Mickelson shot a stunning 65 in the final round, Stenson posted a 63! Stenson became the first Swedish golfer to win a men's major and his score of 264 over four rounds was the lowest ever in a major tournament! The pair started the day one stroke apart and battled back and forth before Stenson put together three straight birdies starting at No. 14. The big blow came on a 51-foot birdie putt on No. 15. In the end, Mickelson added to his 11 runner-up finishes in majors, second-most all-time. The final score by "Lefty" would have won every British Open but two since 1900!

The British Open was the biggest story of the year, but not the only one. Until then, the shocking collapse by **Jordan Spieth** at the Masters had been the big headline. Spieth was Mr. Golf in 2015, winning two

SPECIAL SPIETH
Jordan Spieth wrapped up his amazing 2015 season with a come-from-behind win at the season-ending Tour Championship. That gave him the FedEx Cup and $10 million! As if he needed it! Jordan Spieth won five times on tour in 2015, including the Masters and US Open.

majors and the FedEx Cup (see box). At the 2016 Masters, Spieth held a solid lead in the final round. Then he stunned fans by taking 7 shots on the par-3 12th hole. Suddenly, Englishman **Danny Willett** was in the lead. Spieth never recovered and must have had to hold back tears as he helped Willett, who had just won his first major, put on the winner's green jacket.

At the US Open, another first-time winner emerged. **Dustin Johnson** had come oh-so-close several times to a major win, but finally came through this year. He made a clutch par putt on No. 16, while leader Jason Day made double-bogey on No. 17. For the first time, Johnson then finished off with the win.

The final major made it four in a row for first-time champs. **Jimmy Walker** shot 65 in the opening round, then held off defending-champion (and world No. 1 player) **Jason Day** in a wire-to-wire win.

2016 MEN'S MAJORS
MASTERS	**Danny Willett**
US OPEN	**Dustin Johnson**
BRITISH OPEN	**Henrik Stenson**
PGA CHAMPIONSHIP	**Jimmy Walker**

Chip Shots

Scorecard

In June, the PGA Tour had to cancel the Greenbrier Classic after major flooding covered the course. It was the first tournament cancellation since 2009. The Tour and its players chipped in with funds to help victims of the flooding. . . . The great **Tiger Woods** missed the 2016 golf season after undergoing back surgery. Fans watched impatiently as he tried to get back in shape, but it was taking a long time! . . . In August, **Jim Furyk** became the first PGA Tour player to shoot a 58 for 18 holes. Furyk was already part of the special club of six golfers who had shot 59. Now he stands alone!

Buzz, Buzz

Golf was played in the Olympics for the first time since 1904, but many of the top men's players chose not to play. Most blamed fear of the Zika virus, a disease spread by mosquito bites. Others said it would get in the way of the regular Tour events. On the women's side, though, nine of the top 10 players in the world took part. Find out who won in the Olympics section starting on page 20!

1 Australia's **Jason Day** took over the No. 1 spot in the world rankings for the first time in his career. Winning three times in the first half of 2016 helped a lot!

Happy Hurley! ▲

Billy Hurley III has already had a pretty exciting life. He went to the US Naval Academy and served in the Navy for several years, including service on a huge destroyer. He was also pretty good at golf, and followed his PGA dreams after his active duty time was up. But driving a huge ship proved a bit easier than making tiny putts. Heading into the 2016 Quicken Loans National in June, he was ranked No. 198 on the Tour. But he broke through with his first PGA Tour win at the event, helped by a surprise chip-in on No. 15 on Sunday. How much of a Navy fan is Hurley? He ended one interview on ESPN by saying simply, "Beat Army!"

THANKS, SON!

Every two years, the Presidents Cup matches a US team against a team of non-European international golfers. The US captain in 2015 was veteran golfer **Jay Haas**. He chose PGA pro **Bill Haas**—his son—to be on the team. That turned out to be a winning pick.

Haas blasted the US to a win.

After the first two days of the match, played in South Korea, the score was much closer than expected. The US team had won five straight Presidents Cups, but that streak was in jeopardy, as it headed into the final-day singles matches one point ahead.

On Sunday, **Chris Kirk** earned a key point when he beat India's **Anirban Lahiri**. **Phil Mickelson** and **Zach Johnson** wrapped up unbeaten weeks with wins. But US superstar **Jordan Spieth** suffered a surprising defeat, South Africa's **Branden Grace** finished the week perfect, and the entire Cup came down to the final match.

Bill Haas faced Korean hero **Sangmoon Bae**. The two arrived at the 18th with Haas up one. Then Bae saw his chip roll back down a hill toward his feet and he knew his match and the Cup were lost, 15.5 to 14.5. Haas the dad congratulated Haas the son and the rest of the winning US team.

LPGA 2016

Ko hoisted her second major in 2016.

Youth was the big word on the LPGA Tour in 2016. The great young New Zealand golfer **Lydia Ko** continued an amazing run of golf. In April, she won the ANA Inspiration in California. When she held up the trophy, she was only 18! Add that to her 2015 Evian title and she became the youngest golfer ever with two major championships. That beats the record set by **Young Tom Morris** . . . in 1869!

In June, Ko almost won her third major, but was beaten by another 18-year-old, Canada's **Brooke Henderson**. At the Women's PGA Championship in Washington State, Henderson birdied the first playoff hole to beat Ko. She became the first Canadian winner of a major since 1968. Henderson helped herself with a hole-in-one in the opening round, for which she won a new car! (She gave it to her sister, **Brittany**, who is also her caddie!)

In July, Ko was in the lead after three rounds at the US Women's Open, but made several bogies on the back nine. **Brittany Lang** and **Anna Nordqvist** wound up tied. In the playoff, Nordqvist fell victim to TV replays, which caught her club knocking a few grains of sand in a bunker before she hit the ball. The grains were tiny, but that broke the rules (though she didn't know it or do it on purpose). TV caught the movement, and she got a two-stroke penalty. That helped Lang win her first major.

Ko won the ANA when **Ariya Jutanugarn** bogeyed her final three holes to drop out of the lead. But in July at the Women's British Open, Jutanugarn finished strong. Chasing her first major, she won by three strokes, overcoming **Mirim Lee**, who had shot a record-tying 62 in the opening round. Jutanugarn became first player from Thailand to win a major golf event. Lee tied for second place.

LPGA MAJOR WINNERS

ANA INSPIRATION	**Lydia Ko**
WOMEN'S PGA	**Brooke Henderson**
US WOMEN'S OPEN	**Brittany Lang**
WOMEN'S BRITISH OPEN	**Ariya Jutanugarn**
EVIAN CHAMPIONSHIP	_____

SOLHEIM CUP

A final-day rally earned the US team the Solheim Cup, its first since 2009. The event pits American golfers against a team from Europe and is held every two years. The 2015 event was one of the most dramatic, in more ways than one.

Europe led by four points entering the Sunday matches, but Americans won eight of the 12 singles pairings for a come-from-behind win. **Paula Creamer** clinched the Cup in the final match, defeating Germany's **Sandra Gal**.

The drama had started earlier in the day, however. During fourball play (which matches pairs of golfers), a decision by a Swedish golfer created controversy. In match-play golf, it is typical for opponents to "concede" short putts for each other. That is, the golfers will agree that the putt is good without having to actually hit it. On the 17th hole of her match, American golfer **Alison Lee** picked up her ball, thinking that England's **Charley Hull** and Norway's **Suzann Pettersen** had conceded the putt. Pettersen then claimed they had not conceded it. The umpire awarded the hole to the Europeans, who went on to win the match. Players on both sides were shocked at Pettersen, who seemed to have broken one of golf's unwritten rules. But she stuck to her decision.

Did the controversy give the American team an extra push that afternoon? Whatever it took, the US won the final five singles matches to claim the Cup.

SCORECARD

The youth movement on the LPGA Tour is more than just Ko and Henderson. The first 14 LPGA events of the year were won by players 23 and younger. Three of those went to 20-year-old **Ariya Jutanugarn** from Thailand . . . **Ha Na Jang** of South Korea and **Haru Nomura** of Japan joined Ko as two-time winners in early 2016 . . . **Lexi Thompson** was the top-ranked American golfer on the tour. She was No. 4 worldwide, thanks in part to a win in February in Thailand and five other top-10 finishes . . . **Ko** added a 2016 ESPY Award as the Best Female Golfer at the awards show in June.

Creamer showed All-American style.

The Majors

In golf, some tournaments are known as the majors. They're the most important events of the year on the men's and women's pro tours. (There are four men's majors and five women's majors.) Among the men, **Jack Nicklaus** holds the record for the most all-time wins in the majors. **Patty Berg** won more majors than any other women's player.

MEN'S

	MASTERS	US OPEN	BRITISH OPEN	PGA CHAMP.	TOTAL
Jack **NICKLAUS**	6	4	3	5	**18**
Tiger **WOODS**	4	3	3	4	**14**
Walter **HAGEN**	0	2	4	5	**11**
Ben **HOGAN**	2	4	1	2	**9**
Gary **PLAYER**	3	1	3	2	**9**
Tom **WATSON**	2	1	5	0	**8**
Bobby **JONES**	0	4	3	0	**7**
Arnold **PALMER**	4	1	2	0	**7**
Gene **SARAZEN**	1	2	1	3	**7**
Sam **SNEAD**	3	0	1	3	**7**
Harry **VARDON**	0	1	6	0	**7**

SOLHEIM CUP: ALL-TIME WINNERS

YEAR	WINNING TEAM (SCORE)	YEAR	WINNING TEAM (SCORE)
2015	UNITED STATES (14.5–13.5)	2002	UNITED STATES (15.5–12.5)
2013	EUROPE (18–10)	2000	EUROPE (14.5–11.5)
2011	EUROPE (15–13)	1998	UNITED STATES 16–12
2009	UNITED STATES (16–12)	1996	UNITED STATES (9–7)
2007	UNITED STATES (16–12)	1994	UNITED STATES (13–7)
2005	UNITED STATES (15.5–12.5)	1992	EUROPE (11.5–6.5)
2003	EUROPE (17.5–10.5)	1990	UNITED STATES (11.5–4.5)

WOMEN'S

	LPGA	USO	BO	ANA	EV	MAUR	TH	WES	TOTAL
Patty **BERG**	0	1	0	0	0	0	7	7	15
Mickey **WRIGHT**	4	4	0	0	0	0	2	3	13
Louise **SUGGS**	1	2	0	0	0	0	4	4	11
Annika **SÖRENSTAM**	3	3	1	3	0	0	0	0	10
Babe **ZAHARIAS**	0	3	0	0	0	0	3	4	10
Betsy **RAWLS**	2	4	0	0	0	0	0	2	8
Juli **INKSTER**	2	2	0	2	0	1	0	0	7
Inbee **PARK**	3	2	1	1	0	0	0	0	7
Karrie **WEBB**	1	2	1	2	0	1	0	0	7

KEY: LPGA = LPGA Championship, USO = US Open, BO = British Open, ANA = ANA Inspiration, EV = Evian Championship, MAUR = du Maurier (1979–2000), TH = Titleholders (1937–1972), WES = Western Open (1937–1967)

PGA TOUR CAREER EARNINGS*

1. Tiger Woods $110,061,012
2. Phil Mickelson $81,053,181
3. Vijay Singh $70,504,566
4. Jim Furyk $66,750,292
5. Ernie Els $48,722,269
6. Davis Love III $44,282,764
7. Adam Scott $43,685,424
8. Sergio Garcia $43,598,914
9. Steve Stricker $42,238,069
10. David Toms $41,817,482

LPGA TOUR CAREER EARNINGS*

1. Annika Sorenstam $22,573,192
2. Karrie Webb $19,813,704
3. Cristie Kerr $17,555,284
4. Lorena Ochoa $14,863,331
5. Suzann Pettersen $13,976,590

*Through July 2016

ADAM SCOTT

This Australian player made the biggest move up the money list in the past year. He burst onto the international scene when he won The Players' Championship in 2004. At 23, he was the youngest winner ever of that important event. An up-and-down career followed, with the worst moment coming at the 2012 British Open, which he lost after holding a four-stroke lead with four holes to play. But he bounced back by becoming the first Aussie to win the Masters in 2013. He later briefly held the world No. 1 ranking and remains among the world's best.

TENNIS

FOUR IN A ROW!
By capturing the 2016 French Open, Novak Djokovic became the first man in 47 years to hold all four Grand Slam titles at one time.

Men's Tennis

A year after falling one victory short of the Grand Slam (winning all four major events in a single year), **Novak Djokovic** met a summer surprise that means he'll have to try again in 2017.

Still, the world's No. 1 player had another amazing year. He won the first Grand Slam event of the year, repeating as Australian Open champion by defeating Scotland's **Andy Murray**. Djokovic then added tournament titles at Indian Wells, Miami, and Madrid. Those were a warm-up for the French Open, the only Slam event he did not win in 2015. He did win in 2016, once again defeating Murray. That gave him 12 Grand Slam titles for his career, tied for fourth on the all-time list. It also made him the first male player since **Rod Laver** in 1969 to win four consecutive Grand Slam events.

Wimbledon was next on Djokovic's radar, but he didn't see **Sam Querrey** coming! The American pulled off a huge upset, beating the No. 1 player in an early round. It was Djokovic's first loss in a Grand Slam match after 30 straight wins. Murray took advantage and beat **Milos Raonic**

Murray was king of Wimbledon again.

to win his second championship at the All England Club (to the delight of British fans, including royalty!).

The year wasn't just about Djokovic, however. The Association of Tennis Professionals (ATP) has dozens of events every year around the world. Through the first seven months of 2016, men from 13 different nations had won at least one ATP event. **Kei Nishikori** of Japan, for example, won his fourth consecutive Memphis Open. Clay-court specialist **Pablo Cuevas** of Uruguay won his second straight Brazil Open. Querrey and fellow American **Steve Johnson** also captured tournament titles.

All the players build up points trying to earn a spot in the season-ending ATP World Tour Finals in November in London. Guess who won the 2015 edition of that event? That's right: Djokovic.

2016 MEN'S GRAND SLAMS

AUSTRALIAN OPEN	**Novak Djokovic**
FRENCH OPEN	**Novak Djokovic**
WIMBLEDON	**Andy Murray**
US OPEN	**Stan Wawrinka**

Women's Tennis

The oldest Grand Slam winner looked strong!

"When I was four or five, I turned on the TV, and [Serena and Venus Williams] were playing. Today, I turn the TV on, and they are still playing. So I am saying, 'How is this possible?'"

— GARBIÑE MUGURUZA, BEFORE BEATING SERENA IN THE FRENCH OPEN FINAL

You might think that the great **Serena Williams** doesn't feel pressure. After all, she has held the world No. 1 spot since early 2013! In 2015, she wrapped up her second "Serena Slam," winning four consecutive Grand Slam tournaments (including one in 2014 and three in 2015). But she was shockingly upset at the 2015 US Open. At that point, she needed just one more Grand Slam tournament win to match **Steffi Graf**'s all-time record of 22 in the Open Era. (Margaret Court won 24 titles, but many came before the Open Era started in 1968, when professionals were allowed to compete.) Would Williams get it in 2016? It turned out to be harder than many thought!

An Australian Open title would have done it, but Williams was upset again, this time by **Angelique Kerber** of Germany.

The French Open was next. It's held on clay. That is not Williams's favorite surface, although she has won the French Open three times. She made yet another final, but this time the surprise winner was **Garbiñe Muguruza** of Spain.

Was the pressure of equaling Graf's mark too much for Williams? Some journalists wondered if the chase was getting to her.

Williams answered her critics with a convincing win at Wimbledon. It was her seventh win at the famous tournament, tied for second-most on the all-time list. At 34, she also broke her own record as the oldest woman to win a Grand Slam event. And then she won her 14th Grand Slam doubles title with her sister Venus, who returned to the top 10 in the world.

2016 WOMEN'S GRAND SLAMS

AUSTRALIAN OPEN	**Angelique Kerber**
FRENCH OPEN	**Garbiñe Muguruza**
WIMBLEDON	**Serena Williams**
US OPEN	**Angelique Kerber**

Tennis Notes

LONG TIME COMING

In late 2015, Great Britain won its first Davis Cup in 79 years! The annual tennis tournament among national teams has been around since 1900. Great Britain won several times in the Cup's early days, but not since. That slump ended when Wimbledon champ **Andy Murray** got a big singles win over Belgian **David Goffin**. It gave Britain enough points to win the Cup. "It's one of the highlights of all our careers," Murray said.

EMERGING STARS

In 2016, American tennis fans saw a great trend: rising American female stars! **Sloane Stephens** won events in New Zealand, Mexico, and South Carolina. She was ranked among the top 20 in the world for the first time since 2013. **Madison Keys** won a tournament in England, was runner-up at the Italian Open, and entered the world top 10 for the first time. Thanks to these young stars (and the Williams sisters!), US players won more women's titles than any other nation in 2016.

SURPRISE STAR

Britain's **Marcus Willis** began the week at Wimbledon ranked No. 772 in the world. But he shocked the world by winning six consecutive matches in pre-Wimbledon qualifiers—and by winning at Wimbledon itself! In an early round match, he upset No. 54 **Ricardas Berankis**. Willis was the lowest-ranked player to win a match at Wimbledon since 1988. English fans love an underdog, and he quickly became a crowd favorite. Unfortunately, his Cinderella story ended at the hands of seven-time Wimbledon champ **Roger Federer**. Even after beating the underdog, Federer said, "This story is gold!"

TENNIS FOR ALL

Wheelchair tennis has been part of all the Grand Slam events for some years now, except singles matches at Wimbledon. Matches there are played on grass, and it was thought the surface would not work for rolling wheels. But in 2016, wheelchair singles was held at the All England Club for the first time. It proved to be tougher than the players' usual matches. The grass not only slowed the chairs, but also sped up the ball. The competitors adjusted and played on. Scotland's **Gordon Reid** (right) won the men's title, while **Jiske Griffioen** of the Netherlands won the women's title.

Grand Slams

ALL-TIME GRAND SLAM CHAMPIONSHIPS (MEN)

	AUSTRALIAN	FRENCH	WIMBLEDON	US OPEN	TOTAL
Roger **FEDERER**	4	1	7	5	**17**
Rafael **NADAL**	1	9	2	2	**14**
Pete **SAMPRAS**	2	0	7	5	**14**
Novak **DJOKOVIC**	6	1	3	2	**12**
Roy **EMERSON**	6	2	2	2	**12**
Björn **BORG**	0	6	5	0	**11**
Rod **LAVER**	3	2	4	2	**11**
Bill **TILDEN**	0	0	3	7	**10**
Andre **AGASSI**	4	1	1	2	**8**
Jimmy **CONNORS**	1	0	2	5	**8**
Ivan **LENDL**	2	3	0	3	**8**
Fred **PERRY**	1	1	3	3	**8**
Ken **ROSEWALL**	4	2	0	2	**8**

ROY EMERSON

In 2016, he got company in fourth place on this list, but the powerful Aussie won't lose his place among the all-time greats. He won six Australian Opens (the first was in 1961) and is one of only seven male players to win each of the Grand Slam tournaments at least once. He also won 16 Grand Slam doubles titles and was on eight Davis Cup–winning teams. The International Tennis Hall of Famer is seen regularly at tennis events.

ALL-TIME GRAND SLAM CHAMPIONSHIPS (WOMEN)

	AUSTRALIAN	FRENCH	WIMBLEDON	US OPEN	TOTAL
Margaret Smith **COURT**	11	5	3	5	**24**
Steffi **GRAF**	4	6	7	5	**22**
Serena **WILLIAMS**	6	3	7	6	**22**
Helen Wills **MOODY**	0	4	8	7	**19**
Chris **EVERT**	2	7	3	6	**18**
Martina **NAVRATILOVA**	3	2	9	4	**18**
Billie Jean **KING**	1	1	6	4	**12**
Maureen **CONNOLLY**	1	2	3	3	**9**
Monica **SELES**	4	3	0	2	**9**
Suzanne **LENGLEN**	0	2*	6	0	**8**
Molla Bjurstedt **MALLORY**	0	0	0	8	**8**

*Also won four French titles before 1925; in those years, the tournament was open only to French nationals.

Monica Seles

In the prime of her career, **Monica Seles** was nearly as unstoppable as **Serena Wiliams** has become. From 1991 to 1993, Seles won seven Grand Slam singles titles. She grew up in Yugoslavia, but moved to America when she was 12 and became a citizen. Using a powerful left-handed stroke (and famously grunting loudly as she hit just about every ball), she won her first title when she was 15. Sadly, her career was shortened after she was stabbed on the court by a crazed fan in April 1993. She was away from tennis for two years and, although she won the 1996 Australian Open, never really regained her top form. She was named to the International Tennis Hall of Fame in 2009.

OTHER SPORTS

THAT CHAMPIONSHIP FEELING
In 2016, the University of North Carolina won both the men's and the women's NCAA lacrosse championships. Lacrosse is one of the fastest-growing sports in the country. Millions of young people are picking it up. After UNC's Chris Cloutier (45) scored a game-winner in overtime (see page 180), he celebrated with teammate William McBride.

Winter Sports

World Cup Skiing

American **Lindsey Vonn** has dominated women's skiing for years. About the only thing that has slowed her down is injury. That's what happened in 2015–16. She missed some early races getting over an ankle injury, then could not ski in some later events after she was bitten by her dog! She skied enough to win the downhill championship again but fell short of her fourth overall world title. Vonn reached 76 individual career race wins—the most ever for a woman and second all-time behind **Ingemar Stenmark**'s 86 among all World Cup skiers.

Super G champion **Lara Gut** of Switzerland took advantage of Vonn's absence

WORLD CUP NOTES

✳ In a World Cup slalom event in Colorado in November, American skier **Mikaela Shiffrin** won by 3.07 seconds. That might not seem like a lot, but it was the largest margin of victory ever in World Cup slalom!

✳ In a race in Italy, a drone-carried TV camera almost hit a skier! World Cup officials immediately banned flying robots from future events. Good call!

✳ Austrian skier **Matthias Mayer** was seriously hurt in a crash in Italy. It could have been worse. His new personal air bag safety gear popped open as he crashed. It probably saved him from more severe injuries.

Lara Gut won the overall World Cup championship for the first time.

Figure Skating

American figure skaters had their best showing in a decade, winning two of the top four places at the 2016 World Championships. **Ashley Wagner** finished second, while **Gracie Gold** was fourth. As good as they were, however, they could not overcome a record-setting free-skate performance by **Evgenia Medvedeva** of Russia. Her 150.10 final gave her the world championship over Wagner.

In the ice dance event, Americans won silver (**Maia** and **Alex Shibutani**) and bronze (**Madison Chock** and **Evan Bates**) to bring the team medal total to three. France's **Gabriella Papadakis** and **Guillaume Cizeron** won the ice dance gold.

On the men's side, most eyes were on **Yuzuru Hanyu** of Japan. He was the defending Olympic champ and had set a new free-skate scoring record earlier in the season. However, at the finals, he fell short of **Javier Fernandez** of Spain, who won his second consecutive world championship. Canada's **Meagan Duhamel** and **Eric Radford** won pairs.

A thrilling short program boosted Wagner.

to win her first overall World Cup title. **Eva-Maria Brem**, from Austria, was the giant slalom champ, while Sweden's **Frida Hansdotter** won the slalom. That event might have been another win for American star **Mikaela Shiffrin**, but she, too, missed several races due to injury.

On the men's side, Austria's **Marcel Hirscher** was the big story. He won the giant slalom championship and racked up enough other points to capture the overall World Cup title. That was nothing new for him—it gave him five titles in a row! Italy's **Peter Fill** was the downhill champ. Norwegians **Henrik Kristoffersen** (slalom) and **Aleksander Aamodt Kilde** (Super G) also took home championships. France's **Alexis Pinturault** was the winner in the combined event.

Rugby World Cup

Five points for New Zealand, as Julian Savea dives in during the semifinal.

When just about everyone expects your team to come out on top, it can be almost too much pressure. Just about every expert in the world picked New Zealand to repeat as Rugby World Cup champions. No team had ever accomplished that feat. New Zealand came through, defeating Australia 34–17 in a tough battle in the final. Fly-half **Dan Carter** kicked 19 points to lead the way in his final match for his country. Australia was within 4 points before New Zealand pulled away. Earlier in the 20-team tournament, Japan pulled off what some people called the biggest upset in Rugby World Cup history, beating South Africa 34–32. It was Japan's first win ever in the World Cup . . . and South Africa, a two-time champ, went on to finish third overall! The United States Eagles also were part of the tournament. Rugby is not a big deal in America, of course, but the team was good enough to earn a spot. Unfortunately, the Eagles lost all four of their matches, including a 64–0 thrashing by South Africa (which was mad over losing to Japan earlier in the tournament!).

Cricket World Championships

Imagine that in baseball's World Series, the home team was down by 3 runs in the bottom of the ninth. Then imagine four consecutive batters hitting home runs, the last one giving his team the title.

Something pretty much like that happened at the World T20 cricket championships. The 16-team tournament was held in April 2016; the next won't be until 2020, so it was a huge deal. The T20 version of cricket is played so that matches last only about three hours. Each team faces only 120 pitches, trying to score as many runs as it can. The format has helped make a popular sport even more popular. ("Test" cricket played between national teams usually lasts for five days. Yes, five days!)

The championship of the 2016 World T20 event, held in cricket-crazy India, pitted a team from England against a team representing

Brathwaite made history for the West Indies.

> **This was more than the stuff that dreams are made of. You could not have even dreamed this could happen.**
> — CARLOS BRATHWAITE

the West Indies. Players on that team come from several island nations in the Caribbean.

In T20, each team gets to bat once. England went first and scored 155 runs. The West Indies did well but was trailing as its final batsman stepped in. **Carlos Brathwaite**'s team was down to its final four pitches and was behind by 18 runs. What he did next made cricket history.

Brathwaite hit four consecutive balls out of the park, each worth 6 runs. The final 6 made the West Indies the world champions for the second time.

Lacrosse

MAJOR LEAGUE LACROSSE

Lightning struck twice in the Major League Lacrosse championship game. First, real shocks from the sky postponed the start of the game. Then, with just 13 seconds left, **Eric Law** delivered his own bolt out of the blue. His goal lifted the Denver Outlaws to a thrilling 19-18 win over the Ohio Machine. It was MVP Law's fifth goal of the game, and it gave the Outlaws their second MLL title.

NORTH CAROLINA WINS

Chris Cloutier scored in overtime to give North Carolina its first national title in lacrosse since 1991. The Tar Heels beat Maryland 14–13. North Carolina started the season 3–3 but rallied to make it to the title game. And for the first time since Princeton did it in 1994, UNC won both the men's and the women's titles. The women also beat Maryland in the title game!

◀◀◀ NATIONAL LACROSSE LEAGUE

Saskatchewan's NLL team is called the Rush, but they were in no rush to win their second straight championship. They waited until the final 12 seconds to score the winning goal in a thrilling 11–10 victory over the Buffalo Bandits. **Jeff Cornwall** scooped up a rebound of a shot and raced the length of the field to score the winner. Sasketchewan had won the first of the best-of-three series 11–9 in a game at Buffalo. Hardworking Rush goalie **Aaron Bold** was the MVP of the championship. NLL games are played indoors on hockey-rink-sized fields, with six players on each team. Nine teams play an 18-game season in the United States and Canada. The action is fast and furious, with amazing stickwork, wall passes, and hard hits.

Boxing

After nearly 10 years as the world heavyweight boxing champion, **Wladimir Klitschko** finally lost. British slugger **Tyson Fury** (black trunks) defeated the massive champ in a unanimous decision in Germany. It was only Klitschko's fourth loss to go with 64 wins. Fury, who was named after former world champ **Mike Tyson**, picked up the championship belts awarded by three major international boxing groups. Fury can thank his family for some of his boxing skill—he has relatives on both sides who were bare-knuckle champions long ago. Fury, of course, uses gloves!

Cycling

Chris Froome of Great Britain won his third Tour de France cycling race in 2016, but not without some drama. Froome was leading Stage 12 of the 21-stage race when he crashed. He hit a motorcycle that stopped suddenly because fans had crowded onto the roadway! Froome left behind his broken bike and started running toward the finish line! He eventually got a new bike and finished more than six minutes behind. However, race officials said the crash was not his fault, so they gave him credit for a better time. Froome also survived a crash on a slippery road in Stage 19. A day later, he rode to victory!

Triple Crown Races

In 2015, the horse racing world was thrilled to watch American Pharoah become the first horse in 37 years to win the Triple Crown. Would 2016 see another Triple Crown champ?

MAY 7: Kentucky Derby

With a powerful stretch run, **Nyquist** won his eighth straight race. And it was a big one: the 142nd running of the Kentucky Derby. The most famous horse race in the world kicks off the Triple Crown season. Nyquist became the fourth California-bred horse in five years to win the event. Before that stretch, the Derby was most often won by horses from the East and South. For jockey **Mario Gutierrez**, it was a return to the top. He won the Derby in 2012 on **I'll Have Another**.

MAY 21: Preakness

No Triple Crown winner this year! On a track covered by thick mud, **Nyquist** lost a race for the first time. In the second leg of the Triple Crown, **Exaggerator** spattered through the mud to win. Nyquist led early but couldn't keep up with Exaggerator's final sprint. The Kentucky Derby winner ended up in third.

JUNE 11: Belmont Stakes

The Triple Crown events wrapped up with the most exciting race of the series. Although **Nyquist** did not race in the Belmont Stakes, **Exaggerator** was going for two-thirds of the Crown. But it was not his day, and he finished 11th. Instead, a pair of powerful gray horses battled neck-and-neck on the track in Long Island, New York. **Destin** held a slight lead over **Creator** as they pounded down the homestretch. They flashed across the finish line together. Only a close-up photo showed that Creator had won the Belmont Stakes . . . by a nose!

Nyquist (right) stormed ahead to win the Kentucky Derby.

E-Sports Report

TV and More TV
The big news in E-sports in 2016 was the creation of the ELeague. Tournaments have been popular for a couple of years now, with millions of gamers watching around the world online. Major cable TV networks were paying attention, too, and TBS got in first. It broadcast weekly ELeague events. Twenty-four teams battled in the game Counter-Strike: Global Offensive. Fans picked their favorite teams and tuned in to see if their heroes would come out on top.

The birth of TV-based ELeague is a big step for E-sports.

Big Money!
The money for E-sports continues to go up and up. League of Legends top teams took home more than $2 million, but that's just the beginning. More and more games are being played on a national or international level. The online, card-based game Hearthstone was set to hold its third world championship at the BlizzCon gaming event in the fall of 2016 with the total prize pool a cool $1 million! BlizzCon was also the site of the StarCraft II world championship.

Minecraft at the Movies!
Starting in late 2015, going to the movies meant bringing your laptop! Well, on some visits to the theater, at least. Using new network software, fans can sit in comfy theater seats and play in a giant worldwide Minecraft Super League game. Thousands of gamers pack the theaters to take on challenges, some of which they create themselves. If you're a Minecraft fan, find out if Super League is coming to a theater near you. Just make sure not to get popcorn in your keyboard!

League Continues to Lead
The most popular game among E-sports fans remains League of Legends (LoL), which crowns champions in several seasons throughout the year. One reason the game is so popular is that winning teams are from around the world. Counter Logic Gaming won the Spring 2016 LoL championship in Las Vegas in front of tens of thousands of fans. That team then joined five other highly ranked groups in May at the big Mid-Season Invitational in Shanghai. SK Telecom T1 came out on top there.

Amazing Sports

World Drone Prix ▶▶▶

Yes, racing drones! It was like sci-fi come to life as remote-controlled drones zipped around a custom outdoor track in Dubai. Teams drove their machines through tunnels and around obstacles and tried not to crash! Fans watching on TV and, later, online could see the course from the drone's point of view or watch from above as the speedy craft flew. **Luke Bannister** led a team from England to the championship, pocketing $250,000. Not bad for a 15-year-old!

Please Don't Do This at Home!

If your nickname is "The Mountain," you probably have to eat a lot of food to get that big. For World's Strongest Man athlete **Hafthor Bjornsson** (who is also a TV star!), eating is pretty much like breathing. Bjornsson, who weighs 395 pounds and stands 6 feet 9 inches tall, told his fans that he eats more than 10 times a day. This is what an average day includes:

2 pounds of beef

1 pound of salmon

1 pound of chicken

3 pounds of potatoes

14 eggs

4 bananas and lots of other fruit

A potato-banana-Rice Krispie-almond-berry-peanut butter smoothie

Marathon Surprises

Family and friends of high school runner **Evan Megoulas** waited at the finish line of the half-marathon he was running in Philadelphia. But he didn't show up when the race was over. It turned out that he made a wrong turn! Evan ended up running an entire marathon.

In Alabama, another runner was a big surprise, unexpectedly finishing a half-marathon in seventh place. It was her first time running that distance, and she made good time, even after stopping to sniff a dead rabbit. Oh, did we mention this runner was a dog? She was a bloodhound named **Ludivine**!

A Very Long Row

A group of courageous—and, at the end, very tired—women set a new world record by rowing across the Pacific Ocean. They battled waves, weather, sun, sharks, and blisters to complete the 8,500-mile journey. Leaving from San Francisco, they stopped in Hawaii and Samoa to take on more food and water before finishing in Australia. The adventure took nine months, three more than expected. Their boat, named *Doris*, had room for them to take turns sleeping and eating while they churned through the seas. Three British women—**Laura Penhaul**, **Natalia Cohen**, and **Emma Mitchell**—did the entire trip, while three other women took turns on the fourth oar.

❝I'm so proud that we did this. We stepped on board as teammates, and we stepped off as lifelong friends.❞

– ROWER **LAURA PENHAUL** AFTER COMPLETING THE TRANSPACIFIC ROW WITH HER TEAM

Before they headed across the Pacific, the crew practiced in its boat, named Doris.

NCAA Division I Champs

MEN'S SPORTS
(2015–2016 School Year)

BASEBALL
Coastal Carolina

BASKETBALL
Villanova

CROSS-COUNTRY
Syracuse

FENCING (COED TEAM)
Columbia

FOOTBALL (CFP)
Alabama

GOLF
Oregon

GYMNASTICS
Oklahoma

ICE HOCKEY
North Dakota

LACROSSE
North Carolina

RIFLE (COED TEAM)
West Virginia

SKIING (COED TEAM)
Denver

SOCCER
Stanford

Stanford (left) beat Clemson in soccer.

SWIMMING AND DIVING
Texas

TENNIS
Virginia

TRACK AND FIELD (INDOOR)
Oregon

TRACK AND FIELD (OUTDOOR)
Florida

VOLLEYBALL
Ohio State

WATER POLO
UCLA

WRESTLING
Penn State

WOMEN'S SPORTS
(2015–2016 School Year)

BASKETBALL
Connecticut

BEACH VOLLEYBALL
USC

BOWLING
Stephen F. Austin

CROSS-COUNTRY
New Mexico

FIELD HOCKEY
Syracuse

GOLF
Washington

GYMNASTICS
Oklahoma

ICE HOCKEY
Minnesota

LACROSSE
North Carolina

ROWING
California

SOCCER
Penn State

SOFTBALL
Oklahoma

SWIMMING AND DIVING
Georgia

TENNIS
Stanford

TRACK AND FIELD (INDOOR)
Oregon

TRACK AND FIELD (OUTDOOR)
Arkansas

VOLLEYBALL
Nebraska

WATER POLO
USC

Oklahoma's gymnastics team celebrated after flipping and jumping to the title.

Big Events 2016-17

September 2016

7-18 Paralympic Games
Rio de Janeiro, Brazil

8 Pro Football
NFL regular season begins
with a matchup between the
Panthers and defending-
champion Broncos

10-11 Tennis
US Open finals,
New York, New York

17 Ice Hockey
World Cup of Hockey begins,
Toronto, Canada

21 Basketball
WNBA Playoffs begin
Teams and sites TBA

30- Golf
Oct. 2 Ryder Cup,
Chaska, Minnesota

October 2016

4 Baseball
MLB postseason begins
(Wild Card playoff games,
League Division Series,
League Championship Series,
World Series)

7 Ice Hockey
NWHL regular season begins

8 Swim/Bike/Run
Ironman Triathlon World
Championship, Kailua-Kona,
Hawaii

9-16 Cycling
World Road Cycling
Championships, Doha, Qatar

12 Ice Hockey
NHL regular season begins

25 Basketball
NBA regular season begins

November 2016

6 Running
New York City Marathon

7 Soccer
CONCACAF qualifying
for 2018 World Cup begins

13-20 Tennis
ATP World Tour Finals,
London, England

20 Stock Car Racing
Ford Ecoboost 400, final race
of NASCAR Chase for the
Cup, Homestead, Florida

27 Auto Racing
Abu Dhabi Grand Prix,
final race of Formula 1 season

27 Football
Grey Cup, CFL Championship
Game, Toronto, Canada

December 2016

1–10 Rodeo
National Finals Rodeo,
Las Vegas, Nevada

2–4 College Soccer
Women's College Cup,
Site TBA

2 College Football
Pac-12 Championship Game,
Santa Clara, California

3 College Football

Big Ten Championship Game,
Indianapolis, Indiana

SEC Championship Game,
Atlanta, Georgia

ACC Championship Game,
Charlotte, NC

8–18 Soccer
FIFA World Club Cup, Japan

9–11 College Soccer
Men's College Cup,
Houston, Texas

TBA Soccer
MLS Cup,
Site and date TBA

31 College Football

College Football Playoff
Semifinal; Peach Bowl,
Atlanta, Georgia

College Football Playoff
Semifinal; Fiesta Bowl,
Glendale, Arizona

January 2017

2 College Football
Sugar Bowl, New Orleans,
Louisiana
Cotton Bowl, Arlington, Texas
Outback Bowl, Tampa, Florida
Rose Bowl, Pasadena, California

7–8 Pro Football
NFL Wild Card Playoff
Weekend

9 College Football
College Football
Championship Game,
Tampa, Florida

14–22 Figure Skating
US Figure Skating
Championships,
Kansas City, Missouri

14–15 Pro Football
NFL Divisional Playoff
Weekend

14–29 Soccer
African Cup of Nations,
Gabon

22 Pro Football
NFL Conference Championship
Games

26–29 Action Sports
Winter X Games,
Aspen, Colorado

28–29 Tennis
Australian Open finals

29 Pro Football
NFL Pro Bowl,
Orlando, Florida

29 Hockey
NHL All-Star Game,
Los Angeles, California

February 2017

5 Pro Football
Super Bowl LI,
Houston, Texas

6–19 Skiing
World Alpine Ski
Championships,
Saint Moritz, Switzerland

19 Basketball
NBA All-Star Game,
Site TBA

26 Stock Car Racing
(NASCAR) Daytona 500,
Daytona Beach, Florida

TBA Baseball
Caribbean Series,
Culiacan, Mexico

March 2017

29– Figure Skating
Apr. 2 World Figure Skating
Championships,
Helsinki, Finland

TBA Baseball
World Baseball Classic,
Sites TBA

31– College Basketball
Apr. 2 NCAA Women's Final Four,
Dallas, Texas

April 2017

1, 3 College Basketball
NCAA Men's Final Four,
Glendale, Arizona

3 Baseball
Major League Baseball,
Opening Day

6–9 Golf
The Masters,
Augusta, Georgia

11 Ice Hockey
NHL playoffs begin

May 2017

6 Horse Racing
Kentucky Derby,
Churchill Downs,
Louisville, Kentucky

20 Horse Racing
Preakness Stakes,
Pimlico Race Course,
Baltimore, Maryland

28 IndyCar Racing
Indianapolis 500,
Indianapolis, Indiana

June 2017

3 Soccer
UEFA Champions
League Final,
Cardiff, Wales

10–11 Tennis
French Open,
Paris, France

10 Horse Racing
Belmont Stakes,
Belmont Park,
Elmont, New York

15–18 Golf
US Open Championship,
Erin, Wisconsin

17 College Baseball
College World Series begins,
Omaha, Nebraska

17–27 Sailing
America's Cup finals,
Bermuda

17– Soccer
July 2 Confederations Cup,
Russia

29– Golf
July 2 Women's PGA Championship,
Chicago, Illinois

TBA Basketball
NBA Finals, Sites TBA

July 2017

1 Cycling
Tour de France begins,
Düsseldorf, Germany

11 Baseball
MLB All-Star Game,
Miami, Florida

13–16 Action Sports
Summer X Games,
Minneapolis, Minnesota

13–16 Golf
US Women's Open,
Bedminster, New Jersey

15–16 Tennis
Wimbledon Championships
finals, London, England

20–23 Golf
British Open Championship,
Southport, England

August 2017

4–13 Track and Field
World Championships,
London, England

8 Rugby
Women's World Cup begins,
Belfast, Ireland

10–13 Golf
PGA Championship,
Charlotte, North Carolina

Note: Dates and sites subject to change. TBA: To be announced. Actual dates of event not available at press time.

Produced by Shoreline Publishing Group LLC

Santa Barbara, California

www.shorelinepublishing.com

President/Editorial Director: James Buckley, Jr.

Designed by Tom Carling, www.carlingdesign.com

The *Scholastic Year in Sports* text was written by

James Buckley, Jr.

Editor: **Jim Gigliotti** Fact-checking: **Matt Marini**

Thanks to Maya Frank-Levine, Deborah Kurosz, Emily Teresa, and the superstars at Scholastic for all their gold-medal work! Photo research was done by the author.

Photography Credits